THE

MASONIC LADDER:

OR THE

Nine Steps to Ancient Freemasonry,

BEING

A PRACTICAL EXHIBIT, IN PROSE AND VERSE,

OF THE

MORAL PRECEPTS, TRADITIONS,

Scriptural Instructions and Allegories

OF THE DEGREES OF

ENTERED APPRENTICE, FELLOW CRAFT, MASTER MASON,

MARK MASTER, PAST MASTER, MOST EXCELLENT MASTER, ROYAL ARCH MASON, ROYAL MASTER AND SELECT MASTER,

By JOHN SHERER,

Compiler of the "Masonic Carpets of Blue Lodge, Chapter and Council Masonry," and other Masonic Publications.

CINCINNATI, OHIO:
PUBLISHED BY SHERER & CO.
1866.

TO

The Great Masonic Brotherhood,

"A MULTITUDE, WHICH NO MAN CAN NUMBER, OF ALL NATIONS AND KINDREDS AND PEOPLE AND TONGUES;"

WORSHIPING A COMMON DEITY; JOINING HANDS AROUND A COMMON ALTAR; ENGAGED UPON LIKE DEEDS OF BENEFICENCE ON EARTH, AND CASTING HOPE'S STRONG ANCHOR UPON THE SAME HEAVENLY SHORE;

The Masonic Ladder,

ILLUSTRATING THE THREE GREAT SYSTEMS OF SYMBOLICAL, CAPITULAR AND CRYPTIC MASONRY,

IS MOST RESPECTFULLY AND FRATERNALLY

Dedicated,

BY JOHN SHERER.

PREFACE.

IN presenting a new volume to the Masonic Fraternity, and soliciting their patronage for it, it is incumbent on the compiler to show wherein it differs from, and claims superiority over, other publications already in the market.

The great number of Masons do not sufficiently discriminate between the doctrines, covenants and aims of the different degrees. The Three, Seven, or Nine Degrees, conferred in the various Masonic bodies, are apt to be jumbled up in the minds of their recipients, as though they were only so many sections of the same Degree. The more striking parts of the ceremony are remembered, while the instructions, which give the rational explanations of the emblems, are forgotten. Something, then, is needed which the brother can take home with him and read, to refresh his mind upon what is, in reality, the only practical part of the Masonic institution. For this part the "Monitor" is used, and so far as it goes it supplies that want. But the "Monitor" is not sufficiently diffuse. There is not sufficient latitude given to the historical branch of the subject; nor in the moral application of Masonry is the "Monitor" precise and distinct. Something more has been wanted by generations of Masons, and it is strange that none of the Masonic authors have attempted to supply that want.

"The Masonic Ladder" has been prepared with reference to this very want. It is so arranged that the brother may, by its perusal, recall the more striking parts of the Degrees he has taken; may judge of the extent of his covenants; may understand what bearings the history and geography of the Holy Land have upon the traditions that have been communicated to him; and may trace out to its full extent the excellent morality taught in each Degree. At the same time that "The Masonic Ladder" assists the brother to remount the steps he has taken, and enjoy over again the pleasant thoughts experienced when he first took them, they communicate no secrets to an outsider. Like the Bible itself, which is full of Masonic secrets to the

initiated, "The Masonic Ladder" can not open the way to the arcana of the Order save to those who have once penetrated to them.

The compiler has had able assistance in the preparation of this volume, and all the matter contained in it, whether original or selected, has been re-written and adapted to the plan upon which the book was prepared.

The compiler is so well known as the author and publisher of Sherer's "Masonic Carpets" and "Masonic Degree-Books," that he will be indulged in saying that "The Masonic Ladder" is prepared in strict accordance with those well-known and popular productions. The form of the Emblems, and the order of their arrangement, were guides in combining "The Masonic Ladder," so that the two may go together. Every Lodge that has heretofore purchased a Carpet, or may hereafter supply itself with a Degree-Book, can now have a volume explanatory of it. This is a desideratum long sought for by the Lodges.

CINCINNATI, OHIO, JANUARY, 1866.

THE FIRST ORDER IN FREEMASONRY.

THE SYMBOLICAL DEGREES:

CONSISTING OF

THE ENTERED APPRENTICE,

THE FELLOW CRAFT,

AND

THE MASTER MASON.

THESE three Degrees are conferred, according to the system adopted throughout the Masonic world, in Lodges of Symbolical Masonry. The ballot is taken in the Third or Master Mason's Degree, absolute unanimity being essential to an election. All discipline for vice, immorality, improprieties, and the violation of Masonic laws, originates in this Order of Masonry.

ASK, and ye shall receive;
  SEEK, ye shall surely find;
KNOCK, ye shall no resistance meet,
  If come with ready mind;
For all that ASK, and ask aright,
Are welcome to our Lodge to-night.

Lay down the bow and spear;
  Resign the sword and shield:
Forget the *arts of warfare* here,
  The *arms of peace* to wield;
For all that SEEK, and seek aright,
Are welcome to our Lodge to-night.

Bring hither thoughts of peace;
  Bring hither words of love:
Diffuse the pure and holy joy,
  That cometh from above;
For all that KNOCK, and knock aright,
Are welcome to our Lodge to-night.

ASK help of Him that's high;
  SEEK grace of Him that's true:
KNOCK patiently, the hand is nigh,
  Will open unto you;
For all that ASK, SEEK, KNOCK aright,
Are welcome to our Lodge to-night.

THE ENTERED APPRENTICE.

THE ENTERED APPRENTICE.

Where two or three assemble round
  In work the Lord approves,
His spirit with the group is found
  For 'tis the place He loves:
Be now all hearts to friendship given,
For we, the Sons of Light, are *seven.*

Bring here the Gavel and the Gauge,
  Those implements renowned;
And from each conscience disengage
  The faults that there abound:
Be now afar each folly driven,
For we, the Sons of Light, are *seven.*

Display the Law, the volume grace
  With Compass and with Square;
Illume the tapers in their place,
  And all for work prepare:
We'll please our Master well this even,
For we, the Sons of Light, are *seven.*

Spread o'er us yon rich Canopy,
  Set up the Ladder high,
That angel-visitants may see
  And from their stations fly:
Where Faith, Hope, Charity have striven,
And we, the Sons of Light, are *seven.*

THE ENTERED APPRENTICE.

THE FIRST SECTION.

THE THEORY OF THE DEGREE OF ENTERED APPRENTICE.

THE Degree of Entered Apprentice is the initial letter of the Masonic alphabet, the first round in the ladder of grades, variously numbering three, seven, nine, eleven, twenty-nine, one hundred and twenty-five, or whatever figures the fancy of modern ritualists may assume to embrace all the Degrees of Freemasonry. An Entered Apprentice is a beginner, a neophyte. All that is explained to him in the First Degree must be in the sense of laying down a foundation; for he can have no previous information or instruction upon which to base it.

Yet the Entered Apprentice, in theory, is *already a Mason*, even before he enters the Lodge; that is, he must be already *prepared in heart*, for there is nothing in Masonic science that can do the work of heart-preparation. And the neophyte must have had some exoteric knowledge of Masonry as a public institution, because he is required to declare that "he has long entertained a favorable opinion of it."

The theory which makes the character of the Entered

Apprentice that of "a hewer of wood and drawer of water" does not militate against the fact that to his more advanced brethren he is "not now as a servant, but above a servant, a *brother beloved*."

ASK AND RECEIVE.—The manner of application at the door of God's favor, symbolized in the Closed Door, is described in various passages. God said to Solomon: "Ask what I shall give thee." Elsewhere it is recorded: "Ask for the old paths, where is the good way, and walk therein." "Ask, and ye shall receive, that your joy may be full." "Ask, and it shall be given you; seek, and ye shall find; knock, and it shall be opened unto you." "If any man lack wisdom, let him ask of God that giveth to all men liberally, and upbraideth not; and it shall be given him."

In close connection with the symbolism of the Closed Door is that of the Three Knocks, peculiar to the Masonic Ritual. A splendid genius, now deceased, extending the Masonic theory beyond the vale of time, figures the Grand Master of the Universe standing in the Celestial Orient upon "the appointed day," and giving the Three Knocks which shall summon the sheeted dead. At the first knock, the ground of their interment begins to heave with expectation. All nature is hushed. Earth and heaven await with trembling the consummation. At the second knock, bone comes to his fellow, flesh reclothes them; blood moves once more through the veins, and the dead are ready for the last summons. It falls, and at once the armies of the dead arise, stand erect, facing the East, and listen to the words of their Maker!

RIGHT ANGLES, HORIZONTALS, AND PERPENDICULARS. Every thing in Masonic Science admits of a rational explanation. In truth, Freemasonry is *the perfection of reason.* All its instructions conform to mathematical ideas, and the simplest drawings of *right angles, horizontals,* and *perpendiculars* form emblems of greater significance upon its trestle-board. As the architect would say that "all the parts of his edifice are tested by those three emblems, the *square,* the *level,* and the *plumb,* because they are the instruments by which the *right angle,* the *horizontal,* and the *perpendicular* are made upon his drawing," so in *Freemasonry,* which is but another name for *moral architecture,* all methods of communication known to the ancient Craft are to be subjected to the same tests, and *such as fail are spurious.* Thus these simple emblems, the first upon the trestle-booard, become among the most important. When two persons meet, who are able to recount similar necessities, trials, and successes, what mutual disclosures take place! What trustful communications, what tender sympathy is manifested! Then one soul gushes out and flows over into the other, and time steals rapidly on. Such is the nature of Masonic intercourse between sympathetic hearts.

THE DAGGER.—In the Master Mason's lecture, the emblem of "The Sword pointing to the naked Heart" expresses the judgment reserved to the last day for those who presumptuously sin against God and their fellow-men. The same idea is conveyed, but in a more restricted form, by the emblem of the Dagger. It reminds us that there is an inward monitor, *the conscience,* which will not be silent when the heart has resolved upon sin. A person entering the Masonic institution with a view to betray its secrets and violate its covenants need not think that our Order has no avenger. The voice of God within him is our avenger, and the eternal justice of Him who has wisely permitted the existence of this Society for countless ages speaks even now through that voice to his heart, and will speak in thunder-tones to his guilty soul on the Judgment-day. It needs not that any penalty be inflicted by the Craft upon the betrayer of secrets save the necessary discipline of expulsion. We can leave the guilty in the hands of God, who is the avenger of his own laws.

Nor can the utmost treachery of evil men divulge what it is our interest as a society to preserve. Our secrets are lawful and honorable. They were intrusted in peace and honor to the Masons of ancient times, and they will be so transmitted to the ages to come.

THE APRON.—There are two prominent ideas connected with the Masonic use of the Apron: that of protecting the garments from the defilement of the materials with which the practical builders wrought, and that of the distinguishing mark or badge of the Craft. The first notice in Scripture of an Apron, is where our first parents, having their eyes opened, and seeing themselves naked, sewed together fig-leaves and made themselves aprons. But this was not worn for a purpose analogous to ours. The Masonic Apron is exhibited as a continual memento, both to himself and those around him, that he is under peculiar engagements to keep his conscience void of offense, both to God and man.

But the idea, fully reviewed, becomes still more tender and affecting. The Masonic Apron is not made of material of an ordinary sort, such as is used for garments of warmth, decency, or protection. It is made of *lamb-*

skin, and that only, and it thus incorporates into its real ordinary meaning all that pertains to that Divine emblem of innocence. This makes up one of the finest allegories in Freemasonry, and those members of the Fraternity who are Christians see in their Apron every thing taught in the Altar, the Thorny Crown, and the Cross.

THE TWENTY-FOUR INCH GAUGE.—The proper division of our time involves every thing useful in our life. *Our time is our life;* they expire together. He who wastes the one, wastes the other. Nothing but a systematic distribution of time can accomplish the purposes for which we were placed in this world. A portion for God, a portion for needful avocations, a portion for refreshment and sleep—this is the division that Freemasonry enjoins. It were well for every member of the Craft to resolve, in his moments of prayerful reflection, that he will improve, in the best manner possible, all his leisure moments in growing in morality, and to be daily increasing his moral stature in conformity with the lessons inculcated upon the Masonic trestle-board.

THE COMMON GAVEL.—The necessity of a great and radical removing of those evil things that incrust and encumber the conscience is as great as that of breaking off the outside crust and envelopments from the marble before a perfect statue can be formed. The emblem that suggests this necessity is the Gospel. How greatly the beauty of the immortal soul is disfigured, its usefulness impaired, its happiness destroyed, and the God who made it, dishonored, for want of the proper use of this simple instrument for cleansing, trimming, and lightening the soil!

THE THREE GREAT LIGHTS.—The combination of the

three objects, the *Holy Bible*, the *Square*, and the *Compass*, under this denomination, is not incongruous when the character of the instructions they convey to the Masonic mind is considered. The first guides our *faith*, the second our *works*, the third our *passions*. Belief, labor, spirit—these are the three ideas conjoined in this beautiful trio. It is not the reverence we bear to them as tangible objects that is considered here. The Mason reveres *the Bible;* he does not revere any other tangible object. But these three objects are conjoined here simply as emblems, or moral instructors, teaching great inward lessons by outward forms.

THE THREE LESSER LIGHTS.—Pursuing the imagery employed in the last paragraph, we make the three lesser lights, or mediums through which instruction is conveyed to the Craft, to be the Sun, Moon, and Master of the Lodge. The government of the Master is analogous to that exercised over the day by the Sun, over the night by the Moon—a thought which is amplified in the lectures of the Past Master. Much care is exercised in the ritual of the Entered Apprentice to teach the respect due to the Master of the Lodge, without which, order would be lost and innovations flood the Institution.

THE ALTAR.—As a support to the copy of the Holy Scriptures, which forms so essential a piece in the furniture of the Lodge, the Altar would be a highly conspicuous object, were there no other meaning conveyed by it. As an emblem, however, it calls to mind the piety of Abel, Noah, Abraham, and other Old Testament worthies, who are recorded as the builders of altars. It more particularly suggests a sacrifice of prayer and praise to God.

Prayer.—The motto, "To Labor is to Pray," is most congenial to Freemasonry. Much will be said throughout this volume upon the use of prayer as an essential feature in the rituals of this ancient Institution. At first, man was permitted to converse with his Maker, *face to face.* But since the fall, a new, yet tender mode of communication has been divinely instituted between the soul and its Creator, and this is a fundamental landmark in Masonry.

Faith.—The first of the three principal rounds in the Masonic Ladder is denominated Faith. This is a grace of which the Holy Writings are full. It is the cheer of the sorrowing, and the life of the just. It is the credit we give to the declarations of God, or to the evidences of the facts or propositions presented us in the Bible. The faith, without which we can not please God, combines assent with reliance, belief with trust. True faith involves the forsaking of all known sin, and a cheerful and constant obedience to God's commands.

THE WISE CHOICE OF SOLOMON.

The Entered Apprentice is one who, like the wise king of the line of David, chose the better part.

When in the dreams of night he lay,
  Fancy-led through earth and air,
Whispered from the heavenly way,
  The voice of promise met his ear;
Fancy ceased his pulse to thrill—
  Gathered home each earnest thought—
And his very heart was still,
  Awhile the gracious words he caught.

"Ask me whatso'er thou wilt,
  Fame or wealth, or royal power;
Ask me, ask me, and thou shalt
  Such favors have as none before!"
Silence through the midnight air—
  Silence in the thoughtful breast—
What of all that 's bright and fair,
  Appeared in youth and hope the best?

'T was no feeble tongue replied,
  While in awe his pulses stood:
"Wealth and riches be denied,
  But give me Wisdom, voice of God!
Give me wisdom in the sight
  Of the people thou dost know;
Give me of thyself the light,
  And all the rest I can forego."

Thus, O Lord, in visions fair,
  When we hear thy promise-voice,
Thus like him will we declare,
  That Wisdom is our dearest choice.
Light of heaven, ah, priceless boon!
  Guiding o'er the troubled way;
What is all an earthly sun,
  To His celestial, chosen ray?

Wisdom hath her dwelling reared,
  Lo, the mystic pillars seven!
Wisdom for her guests hath cared,
  And meat, and wine, and bread hath given.
Turn we not, while round us cry,
  Tongues that speak her mystic word;
They that scorn her voice shall die,
  But whoso hear are friends of God.

THE SECOND SECTION.

THE Second Section of the Entered Apprentice's Lecture is explanatory of the first, being directed chiefly to showing how reasonable are all the ceremonies and observances of initiation when properly explained. The greater part of it is esoteric, or private, and, as such, can not be explained to any save those who have regularly entered the portals of the Lodge.

LEBANON, JOPPA, AND MORIAH.—These three localities in the Holy Land are closely combined in the Masonic theory: Lebanon, as the source of the great cedars used in the construction of the Temple; Joppa, as the place of their transhipment; Moriah, on the site upon which the edifice was built. The quarries from which the stone was drawn are supposed to be those found in the northern side of the range of hills on which the city of Jerusalem stands. The following lines express the symbolism which the words in the caption suggest:

Thine in the Quarry, whence the stone
For mystic workmanship is drawn;
    On Jordan's shore,
    On Zarthan's plain,
Though faint and weary, thine alone.
The gloomy mine knows not a ray;
The heavy toil exhausts the day;
    But love keeps bright
    The weary heart,
And sings, I'm thine, and thine alway.

Thine on the Hill, whose cedars rear
Their perfect forms and foliage fair;
    Each graceful shaft,
    And deathless leaf,

Of Masons' love the symbols are.
Thine, when a smile pervades the heaven;
Thine, when the sky 's with thunder riven;
Each echo swells
Through answering hills,
My Mason-prayer; for thee 'tis given.

Thine in the Temple, holy place,
Where silence reigns, the type of peace;
With grip and sign,
And mystic line,
My Mason's love I do confess.
Each block I raise, my friendship grows,
Cemented firmly, ne'er to loose;
And when complete,
The work I greet,
Thine in the joy my bosom knows.

Thine at the midnight, in the cave;
Thine on the floats upon the wave;
By Joppa's hill,
By Kedron's rill,
And thine when Sabbath rest we have.
Yes, yes, dear friend, my spirit saith,
I'm thine until and *after death;*
No bounds control
The Mason's soul,
Cemented with a Mason's faith.

The Setting Maul.—As it is one of the wonders of Divine power, and the fitness of things, that from poisonous and inodorous flowers the insect extracts the purest honey, so it is in the transforming power of Masonic symbolisms to turn this emblem, the Setting Mauls, in itself suggestive of noise and violence, into a sweet emblem of peace. "The house was built of stone, made ready before it was brought thither, so that there was neither hammer, ax, nor any tool of iron heard in the house while it was in building." The analogy between operative and speculative architecture seizes with avidity upon this sublime thought, and peace reigns through all the chambers of the Temple of Freemasonry.

"I will give peace in the land," promised Jehovah to his people, while yet in the wilderness, "and none shall make you afraid." "Behold I give unto him my covenant of peace." "There is peace to thee, and no hurt." "The Lord will bless his people with peace." "Glory to God in the highest, and on earth peace."

Such are the thoughts suggested by the Setting Mauls. At the period of the temple-building, universal peace reigned throughout the earth, and thus the materials for building and adorning, which were brought from the utmost parts of the world, were readily collected. It is only in a time of peace that Freemasonry can flourish.

THE SHOE.—The Shoe was ever an emblem of significance in Freemasonry. To remove the Shoe, as Moses was commanded to do before the Burning Bush, and as Joshua was commanded before Jericho, was a token of reverence. The High-Priest in the Temple went barefoot, as a mark of Divine respect. The removal of the Shoe was also a token of humiliation and subjection, as when David fled before Absalom, and Isaiah walked barefoot for three years, and Ezekiel walked barefoot upon a certain occasion. Hence, the expression in Psalm cviii, "Over Edom will I cast out my shoe," imports the subjugation of the country over which the shoe is cast.

All these ideas are embraced, to a greater or less degree, in the Masonic use of the Shoe as an emblem.

The plucking off one's shoe, and giving it to another, was a significant token of a surrendered right of privilege, and this is more directly the Masonic idea. It is this which is expressed in the following lines:

Take this pledge; it is a token
Of that truth which ne'er was broken—
Truth, which binds the mystic tie
Under the All-seeing Eye.

Take this pledge; the ancient brother
By this type bound every other,
Fondly, firmly; death alone
Rends the bond that makes us one.

Take this pledge; the type so lowly
Is, of all our symbols, holy;
'T is Divine; it tells of One,
Gives the raindrops and the sun.

Take this pledge; the token sealeth
All the Judgment-day revealeth;
Honor, truth, fraternal grace
In thy hands with this we place.

The Cable-Tow.—The explanation of this emblem is that of the covenant or tie that binds Masons to each other and to the institution. That this tie must be one of much *strength*, is evidenced by the great antiquity of the Masonic Order, and the firmness with which its members, in all ages, have resisted every allurement to betray their trust. Scriptural quotations convey the spirit of this emblem: "Draw me not away with the wicked." "Draw me, and we will run after thee." "No man can come to me, except the Father, which hath sent me, draw him." "If any man draw back, my soul shall have no pleasure in him." "We are not of them who draw back unto perdition."

The extent or reach of the Masonic covenants, represented by the Cable-Tow, is well expressed in the monitorial explanation of *the extent of the Lodge.* It reaches as far as *to heaven*, suggesting our duty to God; as far as the utmost bounds of *the habitable earth*, suggesting our duty to our fellow-men; as far as the inmost recesses of our *own hearts*, suggesting our duty to ourselves.

> There is a *cord* of length,
> There is a *chain* of strength—
> Around you each I see the sacred coil;
> *How long*, ah, well I know;
> *How strong*, your deeds do show
> The while you labor in the sacred toil.

THE DAGGER.—Our remarks upon a preceding emblem, the SETTING MAULS, are partly applicable here. Although the Dagger is a warlike weapon, yet, as a Masonic emblem, it has its application, in a gentle and pacific character. It suggests the quiet conscience, which results from a sense of Masonic covenants kept and duties done. This inward monitor, *the conscience*, which is the terror of the wicked, is the sweetest companion of the virtuous mind. Paul wrote to his converts, "Our rejoicing is in this, the testimony of our conscience;" and, again, "We trust we have a good conscience in all things, willing to live honestly." In an address he says, "Herein do I exercise myself to have always a good conscience, void of offense toward God and toward men." "They being convicted by their own conscience, went out one by one," is the description of a scene in which the Scribes and Pharisees of olden time figured. Cain, after the cruel blow fell which deprived him of his brother, was convicted by the voice of his own conscience. The further application of this emblem may be seen under the same head upon a preceding page.

THE JOINED HANDS.—This is an emblem of Fidelity, an ingredient in the Masonic cement without which the walls of the institution would speedily crumble and fall. As an emblem, it was well known to the first painters and sculptors of antiquity. Jonathan and David exemplified this principle in a remarkable degree. He alone who is capable of genuine friendship can appreciate the happiness of reciprocating tokens of fidelity with those who are deserving of confidence.

The right hand, which is the instrument of mechanical activity and of strength, is also the seat of Fidelity. "Thy right hand, O God," saith the Prophet of Abarim, "is become glorious in power." "From the Lord's right hand went a fiery law for them." "Thy right hand," says the Psalmist, "hath holden me up. Save with thy right hand, O Lord!"

The use of the right hand, through all the grades of Freemasonry, is peculiarly impressive. It combines the idea of strength with that of love. Taking the candidate by the right hand is an assurance of protection, of brotherly guidance, of brotherly affection. It, in effect, says to him, that the security of the Craft is around him, the banded strength of the Lodge defends him, and the esteem and love of all hearts are secured unto him, so long as he remains faithful to his trust.

THE LAMB.—In our paragraph upon the Apron, in a preceding page, we remarked that the most tender and beautiful thought connected with its symbolism is, that the Masonic Apron is made of lamb-skin alone. This emblem of innocence is so peculiarly appropriate, that even the Messiah himself condescended to represent his own spotless nature under the figure of a Lamb. One of the older prophets prefigures his death in the words, "He was led like a lamb to the slaughter." There is no passage in the Bible more affecting than this. In contemplating the Masonic emblem, the Lamb, the mind is suspended in solemn rapture between earth and heaven. A pacific temperament steals over the soul, and while we admire the tender and submissive nature of this gentle tenant of the field, we are taught what must be our own character if we would attain to that perfection of which Freemasonry teaches. Thus the very clothing of the Freemason, like the symbolical garments which covered the Priest under the typical law, is suggestive of the highest graces and virtues of our profession.

FRIENDLY ADVICE.—An old author proffers some advice to gentlemen who may be inclined to become Masons, of which the following is a synopsis: "When you intend to become a Freemason, go with your friend to the hall where the Lodge is held, and examine the Charter or Warrant under which the Lodge is held. See that it is written or printed on parchment, signed by some Grand Master, Deputy Grand Master, Grand Wardens, and Grand Secretary, and sealed with the Grand Lodge Seal; appointing certain persons named therein, with their successors, to be Master and Wardens; authorizing them to congregate and hold a Lodge, and therein make and admit Freemasons according to ancient custom. Then call for the By-Laws, and having seriously perused them, consider whether your natural disposition will incline you to be conformable to them. Next call for the List of Members, where you may find the names of some of your most intimate and esteemed friends, and perhaps the names of some you would not wish to associate with. If these researches prove agreeable, you may then venture to sign a petition for initiation, lay down your deposit-money, and await with patience the result."

THE THIRD SECTION.

THE Third Section of the Entered Apprentice's Lecture presents full details of the organization, fitting up, and history of the Lodge. The greater part of it is exoteric, and as such, may be explained to any inquirer, though even those passages that seem to have the least mystery about them are parts of the unwritten history of the Order, and can only be perfectly understood by the initiated.

CONSTITUTION OF THE LODGE.—To avoid those irregularities which would result upon the indiscriminate meetings of Masons, and the unrestricted working up of materials into the Lodge, it has been wisely ordained that no assemblage of the Craft can be opened with Masonic form, unless the presiding officer shall be furnished with a charter or warrant from the Grand Lodge possessing jurisdiction, empowering such an act. This is the source of *temporal authority*, and suggests a careful attention to *forms*. In addition to this, there must likewise be a copy of the Holy Scriptures. This is the source of *Divine authority*, and suggests a careful attention to *principles*. With this copy, there must be the essential accompaniments of the Square and Compass, admonishing the circle of laborers of the necessity of squaring their actions and circumscribing their passions. This suggests a careful attention to *self-discipline*, without which the workings of Freemasonry were as a sounding brass and a tinkling cymbal.

Not less than seven members constitute a Lodge in this degree, and any assemblage not in accordance with all the requirements upon this page, that ventures to open a Lodge in Masonic form, is *clandestine*, and comes under the ban of the Craft universal.

ANCIENT MEETING-PLACES.—In days of old, the meetings of the Masonic Craft were held upon the summits of hills, or in crypts at their bases. This was for purposes of seclusion, which is essential to the Masonic work. Hills and dales were accounted sacred places; men thought themselves nearer God there than elsewhere. The law was given to Moses upon a mountain summit, nine thousand feet high. Some of the most affecting scenes between King Solomon and his builders occurred in the crypts beneath Mounts Moriah and Sion. The great sacrifice for sin, which terminated the Mosaic dispensation of rites and ceremonies, occurred upon Calvary, which is a part of the mountain range on which the city of Jerusalem stands.

In modern times an attempt is made to express this symbolism by holding Lodge-meetings in the highest apartments of an edifice. Then there is nothing intervenes between the covering of the Lodge—on which heavenly bodies are depictured—and the great canopy alluded to below, in which the heavenly bodies shine. No eyes look down upon the Mason-work but the eyes of angels deputed as ministering spirits to minister for them who shall be heirs of salvation, and the All-seeing Eye, which pervades the inmost recesses of the human heart.

EXTENT OF THE LODGE.—The limits of the mystical Lodge are the cardinal points; nothing less will satisfy the expansive nature of the principles inculcated in this system. The apartment in which Masons assemble is symbolical of the universe, illimitable on every side, the proper temple of Deity, whose center is every-where, whose circumference is nowhere. To an entering Mason, it is the world in miniature.

Wherever man is tracing
  The weary ways of care,
'Midst arid deserts pacing,
  Or land of balmy air,
We surely know each other;
  And with our words of cheer,
The Brother hails his Brother,
  And hope wings lightly there.

Wherever tears are falling,
  The soul's December rain—
Or heavy sighs are calling
  To human hearts in vain;
Wherever prayer is spoken,
  In earnestness of faith,
And we perceive the token
  That tells our Master's death;

Wherever man is lying,
  Unnoticed and unknown,
Uncared-for in his dying,
  Unheard in cry and groan,

We surely know each other;
  And with our words of cheer,
The Brother hails his Brother,
  And hope wings lightly there.

Supports of the Lodge.—The three foundation-stones upon which the structure of speculative Masonry was originally laid were entitled Wisdom, Strength, and Beauty. These were well named: for there was Wisdom to conceive the plan above all others practical; there was Strength to execute the plan above all others complicated and laborious; and there was Beauty to adorn the plan above all others capable of receiving the elegancies of thought. It were almost superfluous to comment upon these three words, Wisdom, Strength, and Beauty. "Happy," said the wisest of men, "is the man that findeth wisdom—better than silver and gold, more precious than rubies. Length of days is in her right hand, and in her left hand riches and honor. Her ways are ways of pleasantness, and all her paths are peace." "In Gibeon the Lord appeared to Solomon and said, Ask what I shall give thee; and Solomon said, Give thy servant an understanding heart."

Let those who deny that Wisdom is evinced in the structure of Freemasonry, explain, if they can, the exceeding Strength with which it has defied the influences of time and the oppositions of evil men. Let them explain the Beauty with which it stands before the world, the most perfect specimen of moral architecture extant, the most popular institution, the most highly respected in its membership, and the only esoterical system upon earth that has not yielded to the prying eyes of an inquisitive age.

Covering of the Lodge.—In a preceding paragraph allusion is made to the fact that Lodges seek an upper chamber for their places of assemblage, so that there may be nothing interposed between them and the celestial concave, save their own ceiling, upon which are figured the heavenly bodies. In the symbolisms of the Masonic institution, the covering of the Lodge is the starry-decked canopy, the nearest representation of the heavenly home beyond which is afforded in this life. Every object in a Mason's Lodge points to this. The hopes, watered and fed by the inculcations of the lectures, will have their fruition only in this. To the happy land, veiled by the resplendent curtain above, he strives to approach by a Ladder, seen by the sleeper upon Bethel's pillar, when in his lonely slumber God vouchsafed to him a vision. The assent by grades agrees with our own consciousness of weakness. There are many steps, intentionally made short and easy, to conform to human weakness, and every meeting of the Lodge affords us new encouragement to advance along the ascending way. Three of the steps, Faith, Hope, and Charity, are more distinctly marked than the others; and happy the man who places his feet successively upon them. Firmly planted upon the third, the canopy of heaven is not far distant, which being drawn aside by an angel's hand, the flight is ended, the aspirant has his reward!

Furniture of the Lodge.—In subsequent pages of this volume, much space is devoted to the Furniture of the Sanctuary in the wilderness and that of the Temple of Solomon. These were elaborate, costly, and emblematical of all the purposes of the Mosaic dispensation. The Furniture of the Masonic Lodge is more simple, yet equally expressive—it is the Holy Bible, Square, and Compass. In the first section of this Lecture these objects are merely described as emblems, but in the present connection they have a higher meaning. The precepts and examples contained in the volume thus used to *furnish* the Lodge are held in highest veneration. He who esteems them not, is ignorant and unworthy of our companionship. It is at once a guide through the present world and a passport to that which is to come. A terrible denunciation has been threatened to him who shall add to or diminish from the matter which the finger of God has placed there. It is dedicated to God in the threefold division of the Masonic Furniture.

The Square will have ample elucidation in other portions of this volume; and it only needs here to say, that, in the proper distribution of the Lodge Furniture, it is dedicated to the Master of the Lodge, as the Compass is to the Members: the Square teaching official responsibility, the Compass individual regulation of desires and due circumspection of passions.

ORNAMENTS OF THE LODGE.—As one of the three principal supports of the Lodge is termed Beauty, it is analogous to this that there should be Ornaments of the Lodge. These are the Mosaic Pavement, the Indented Skirting that surrounds the Pavement, and the Star in its center. These, like all other Masonic objects, are emblematical of moral and religious instructions. It has already been said that the apartment in which Masons assemble represents the moral universe; the very floor of it suggests the course of human life, checkered with good and evil. One who enters it is reminded, in that epitome of his own career, of the vicissitudes that are both before him and behind him. If he is in a condition of *distress*, he derives comfort from the reflection that he is surrounded with white squares; if in a condition of prosperity, he is taught to be humble, in view of the darker passages of life, to which his very next step may expose him.

The Border, or Skirting, is an emblem full of hope to those who trust, as all Masons profess to do, in God; it prefigures the blessings that are derived from a steady dependence upon Divine Providence, which has its reference in the Star that gleams in the center. To such of the Craft as blend their hopes of bliss in Jesus, the Son of God, this combination of emblems suggests the sublimest aspirations.

Lights of the Lodge.—The emblems representing the sources of Masonic light, or rather the mediums through which Masonic instruction is directly conveyed to the membership, are called Lights. They represent the Master and the two Wardens, who are the windows through which the lights of tradition, revelation, and the Grand Lodge having jurisdiction, can reach the minds of the Craft. This is but an extended reference of the thought conveyed in our elucidation of the Lesser Lights in a preceding page. The situation of these lights corresponding with those of the principal officers of the Lodge, refers the mind to traditions of the Tabernacle and the Temple, which are esoteric; also to the course of the sun through the heavens.

Jewels of the Lodge.—By the term Jewel, we imply whatever is esteemed most precious among us, and displayed as such to represent the abounding wealth of the Institution. Morality, Equality, and Rectitude of Life, for instance, are three moral treasures, which have their emblems in the Square, the Level, and the Plumb. The rude material in the quarry of human life, though incrusted with many excrescences, is yet precious as affording us objects for our moral work, and this is represented by the Rough Ashlar. The same material, when fitted by Divine Grace and the practice of all virtues for the Temple above, is typified by the Perfect Ashlar; while the Book of God, read in nature and revelation, from which we derive all necessary *degree* instruction while upon earth, is represented by the Trestle-board. These three symbols are happily selected and happily named Jewels.

Who wears THE SQUARE upon his breast,
Does in the eye of God attest,
  And in the face of man,
That all his actions do compare
With the Divine, th' unerring Square—
  That squares great virtue's plan:
That he erects his Edifice
By *this design*, and *this*, and *this!*

Who wears THE LEVEL, says that pride
Does not within his soul abide,
  Nor foolish vanity;
That man has but a common doom,
And from the cradle to the tomb,
  A common destiny:
That he erects his Edifice
By *this design*, and *this*, and *this!*

Who wears THE G; ah, type divine!
Abhors the atmosphere of sin,
  And trusts in God alone;

His Father, Maker, Friend, he knows—
He vows, and pays to God his vows,
  As by th' Eternal throne:
And he erects his Edifice
By *this design*, and *this*, and *this!*

Who wears THE PLUMB, behold how true
His words, his walk! and could we view
  The chambers of his soul,
Each thought enshrined, so pure, so good,
By the stern line of rectitude,
  Points truly to the goal:
And he erects his Edifice
By *this design*, and *this*, and *this!*

Thus life and beauty come to view,
In *each design* our fathers drew,
  So glorious, so sublime;
Each breathes an odor from the bloom
Of gardens bright beyond the tomb,
  Beyond the flight of time:
And bids us build on *this* and *this*,
The walls of God's own Edifice!

SITUATION OF THE LODGE.—The Lodge is situated due east and west. All knowledge emanated from the east. Mankind originally emigrated from the east. The Hebrews used the word East to describe all the countries or provinces lying around and beyond the rivers Tigris and Euphrates, or east or north-east of Judea. The expression in Genesis, "from the east," denotes the country east or south-east of Mount Ararat. In traveling from the foot of that mountain to the plain of Shinar, the descendants of Noah would pass southerly on the eastern side of the mountains of Media till they came opposite to Shinar, or to a point north-east of Babylon, from which, by a direct western course, they would pass into Assyria and the plain of Shinar. This is said to be the usual caravan route to this day.

The Tabernacle in the Wilderness was set east and west; so was the Temple of Solomon. The walls formerly inclosing that edifice are proofs of this, corresponding in their present direction with the cardinal points. The miraculous blast by which the Red Sea was opened before the feet of the Israelitish host, blew from the east. The bodies of the Masonic dead are buried due east and west.

DEDICATION OF THE LODGE.—While the central figure in the Lodge, the Holy Scriptures, is dedicated to Him from whom it came, the Lodge itself, with all its furniture, surroundings, and labors, is dedicated to one of two Sainted Patrons of Masonry, men who in their day exemplified the higher graces taught in the lectures—Saint John the Baptist and Saint John the Evangelist. The elder of these was sent from God to announce the coming of Jesus Christ. The other was called, by the commanding voice of Jesus, to leave the humble avocation in which he had been reared, and go out into the world as an evangelist. Whatever virtues of courage, perseverance, obedience to God's Word, and unswerving fidelity that either of these Masonic patrons displayed, is adopted among the treasures of the Lodge. It matters not whether the apocryphal statements which make these men to have been Masons are true or false, it is enough to know that their moral labors were our moral labors, their victories over sin were our victories, and the bright world gained by their perseverance in a good cause is the same wherever the Supreme Architect presides, and where there are "many mansions" remaining for us. In the mean time, it is safe to aver that no deed whose character would have prevented either of these two men from engaging in it, is suitable to us, who have dedicated our Lodge and its labors to them.

TENETS OF MASONRY.—It is but the summing up of what has already been repeatedly intimated in these pages, to say that the tenets of Masonry are Brotherly Love, Relief, and Truth. Being so great a family of men, of all countries and conditions, there is no cement would hold together such a band save that of Love. Being mutually interested in each other's welfare, it requires no law to compel us to look after the wants of such of the band as are sick, solitary, or in distress. The grand aim of the institution is best expressed in the charge given to the members, "to soothe the unhappy, sympathize with their misfortunes, compassionate their miseries, and, as far as in us lies, restore peace to their troubled minds." Our friendships are formed and our connections established upon this basis.

The first and greatest lesson communicated to each initiate is *Truth*, to be a good man and true; true to God, true to the institution, true to his country, true to himself. Hypocrisy and deceit are abhorrent to the good Mason. The volume upon our altar is the Book of Truth. One reason for the peculiarly strong engagements under which the initiate is placed to preserve the essential merits of Freemasonry is, that by his fidelity in this lesser trust, the brethren may judge of his ability to hold fast the truth in all the greater relations of life and of eternity.

CARDINAL VIRTUES OF MASONRY.—The distinction between the *tenets* and the *virtues* of Masonry is barely sufficient to make an easy grade in the moral assent. Temperance, Fortitude, Prudence, and Justice are judicious selections from those classes of merits so abundantly developed in the Scriptures. It is both our duty and our happiness, our labor and our reward, to cultivate Temperance; the want of it unfits the initiate for usefulness and honor among the Craft, and renders him liable to the worst indiscretions. That mental stability which sustains with manly composure the evils of life, and enables a man to resist every proposal to do wrong, is Fortitude. Prudence stands at the helm, while Fortitude buffets the tempest, and thus the voyage is made secure. "If thou faint in the day of adversity," said our First Grand Master, "thy strength is small; the prudent man dealeth with knowledge, but the fool layeth open his folly." One of the most earnest of Evangelists said, "Every man that striveth for the mastery is temperate in all things." As the three virtues above named relate to our self-government, and the usefulness accruing therefrom, Justice, the last of the four, advises us in our dealings with others. The Lord, speaking through Moses, admonished his people in the wilderness: "That which is altogether just shalt thou follow, that thou mayest live;" and he promises that "the just shall live by faith."

MASONIC SERVICE.—The manner of Masonic service is finely represented by the emblems of chalk, charcoal, and clay, the last in this section. From the lessons of antiquity we derive instruction in every step up the mystic Ladder. At this point we may know that the characteristics of our ancient brethren in their relations to their Masters were freedom, fervency, and zeal. Their freedom of service was manifest by night as by day, and they gave off their good works as generously as the rose-leaf its odor. Their fervency of service was like that of the meridian sun itself. Their zeal emulated that of the fertile soil, which in the most inclement season is preparing itself, through the hidden agencies of nature, for the work of production. Without such manner of service the great Temple could not have been completed in one ordinary generation. It was because heart and soul were thrown into the handiwork, that such a piece of perfection was begun and finished within the lifetime of a child. God was honored, not only in the work, but in the manner of it, and for thousands of years the story of the great Temple has perpetuated the freedom, fervency, and zeal of its builders.

Concluding Remarks upon the Scriptures.—The value of the Scriptures and the duty of perusing them appear from many considerations. We may estimate the character and tendency of Divine revelation by contrasting the condition of countries where its true light shineth with that of other countries to which its beams have not extended. The heathen world is large enough, surely, for experiment. In many of its territories the richest blessings of sun and soil are enjoyed in abundance, and there external nature presents itself in its stateliest and loveliest forms; but where are the beauties of holiness? where the fruits and flowers of moral culture? Or if these are disparaged in comparison with intellectual stature and idolized genius, where are the distinguished philosophers and orators, historians and poets of pagan communities? Amidst numberless diversities of condition, they seem to have only this in common to explain their wretchedness, that they want those oracles of God which have been committed unto us; and the conclusions appear fairly deducible that it is, in the absence of the Scriptures, the people are there destroyed for lack of knowledge; that spiritual ignorance, in addition to its proper maladies, has there entailed civil and mental prostration; and that scoffers in our native land owe to the emancipating influence of God's Word that very freedom of thinking which, with ungrateful and impious hand, they wield for the overthrow of its doctrines and institutions.

If we confine our attention to those countries which possess the Word of God, a comparison between that portion of the community by whom the Scriptures are perused, and that portion by whom they are neglected, will conduct us to a like conclusion. No doubt external propriety may, in many instances, be promoted by the simple circumstance of dwelling among Christians who are "living epistles of Jesus Christ, known and read of all men;" and it is not less certain that many may consult the records of truth, and yet hold the truth in unrighteousness. But these apparent exceptions do not invalidate the general and incontestible fact that the classes most conversant with God's Word are most distinguished for the graces which it inculcates; while they who consort with thieves, and partake with adulterers, who give their mouth to evil, and frame deceit with their tongue, are the wicked, who hate instruction and cast God's Word behind them.

These thoughts, from the pen of a learned divine, are

applicable to Masonry, a system founded upon the Bible and dependent upon the revealed Word of God for all its virtuous principles and inculcations.

The effects marked above, as resulting upon the free spread of the Scriptures, are also manifest upon the operations of Freemasonry. Wherever a well-conducted Lodge is planted, its membership being chosen by the cautionary landmarks of the institution, and governed by its moral and spiritual code of laws, a general improvement is visible throughout the community. The vices of theft, debauchery, intemperance, profanity, Sabbath-breaking, and irreligion are much lessened, while the positive virtues of charity, self-control, and attention to religious duties are proportionally advanced. This phenomenon is not apparent upon the operations of any other society, within our knowledge, outside of the Church; and were there no other evidences of the merits of this ancient institution, this, that it produces many of the best fruits of the Bible, would be sufficient to recommend it to all thoughtful persons.

THE FELLOW CRAFT.

THE FELLOW CRAFT.

This Lodge of Five from Tyre came,
Their leader one of matchless fame;
All through the toiling seasons seven,
Their time upon this work was given.

This Lodge of Five from Joppa's shore
To Sion's hill have journeyed o'er;
The quarry's inmost crypt have traced,
Whence many a stone the wall has graced.

This Lodge of Five have reared the shaft
That on the eastward hails the Craft;
And well they know each mystic line
That sanctifies the great Design.

This Lodge of Five with faith obey
The holy Law and holy Day,
And humbly bow when'er they see
The emblem of the Deity.

This Lodge of Five, for honest toil,
Good wages have, Corn, Wine, and Oil;
And should a brother be in want,
They ne'er forget the covenant.

This Lodge of Five have nearly done
The glorious work so long begun,
And homeward-bound they soon will see
The Master in eternity.

THE FELLOW CRAFT.

THE FIRST SECTION.

THE THEORY OF THE DEGREE OF FELLOW CRAFT.

THE Degree of Fellow Craft represents the Entered Apprentice *complete*. It is not merely the second grade in the series; all that is to follow does not express so great an advance from the Degree of Fellow Craft, as that of the Fellow Craft is from the Entered Apprentice. The candidate is no longer a beginner, working without wages, forbidden to look into the plans and drawings of the work, excluded from consultations, without a foundation, but a Fellow-workman with the best; paid an honest stipend, invited to give counsel upon questions of architectural difficulty, and assisted to build up a reputation, in which all the Craft will take a brotherly interest.

As, therefore, large privileges are conferred upon the Fellow Craft, so heavier responsibilities accumulate upon him. Covenants of power restrain him, duties are enjoined upon him, which require industrious application of the best lessons learned in the preceding grade; and, above all, he is taught to reverence the name of Him from whom cometh every good and every perfect gift.

THE ALTAR.—The name of the Altar erected by Moses to commemorate his victory over the Amalekites at Rephidim, was *Jehovah-nissi*, signifying "the Lord, my Banner." This title is equally appropriate to the Masonic Altar. "The Lord is the banner," or standard, of the institution in a peculiar sense; and the Altar, which is the most conspicuous object in the Lodge, is used to uphold His Word before the eyes of the Craft. According to the Mosaic code, "whatsoever touched the Altar must be holy;" and this, again, applies with great force to the Masonic system, whose offerings are the most sound gifts in the power of man to bestow. The poet says:

"Upon the sacred Altar lies,
Ah! many a precious sacrifice,
Made by these working men;
The passions curbed, the lusts restrained,
And hands with human gore unstained,
And hearts from envy clean."

All contained in the Masonic covenants, whether affirmative or negative, whether in the nature of duties or restrictions, are so many sacrifices made for God and in the name of God. He alone who can communicate saving efficacy to any means of doing good, has commanded his blessing from on high upon the sacrifices made on the Masonic Altar, and so may he ever do!

PRAYER.—The view of the Masonic Altar always suggests Prayer as well as sacrifice. The introduction of Prayer as an essential portion of the Masonic drama is so general, that the Verbal Landmark declares, "No man should ever enter upon any great and important undertaking without first invoking the blessings of Deity." Prayer, as understood in the Masonic theory, is the application of want to Him who only can relieve it; the voice of sin to Him who only can pardon it. It is the urgency of poverty, the prostration of humility, the fervency of penitence, the confidence of trust. It is not eloquence, but earnestness; not the definition of helplessness, but the feeling of it; not figures of speech, but compunction of soul. It is the "Lord save us, we perish," of Peter—the cry of faith to the ear of mercy. Adoration is the noblest employment of created beings; confession the natural language of guilty creatures; gratitude the spontaneous expression of pardoned sinners.

Prayer is desire. It is not a conception of the mind, nor a mere effort of the intellect, nor an act of the memory; but an elevation of the soul toward its Maker, a pressing sense of our own ignorance and infirmity, a consciousness of the perfection of God, of his readiness to hear, of his power to help, of his willingness to save. It is not an emotion produced in the senses, nor an effort wrought in the imagination; but a determination of the will, an effusion of the heart. Prayer is the guide to self-knowledge, by prompting us to look after our sins, in order to pray against them; a motive to vigilance, by teaching us to guard against those sins which, through self-examination, we have been enabled to detect.

Prayer is an act both of the understanding and of the heart. The understanding must apply itself to the knowledge of the divine perfections, or the heart will not be led to the adoration of them. It would not be a reasonable service were the mind excluded. It must be *rational worship*, or the human worshiper would not bring to the service the distinguishing faculty of his nature, which is reason. It must be *spiritual worship*, or it would want the distinctive quality to make it acceptable to Him who has declared that he will be worshiped in spirit and in truth.

Prayer is a privilege with which God has favored us, and a necessary part of that obedience which he has required of us to "pray without ceasing; in every thing by prayer and supplication with thanksgiving, letting our requests be made known unto God."

THE SQUARE.—In all languages, the idea Masonically conveyed by this emblem has an expression. The poet has done for the Masonic Order what was desired, in the following lines:

We meet upon the Level and we part upon the Square;
What words of precious meaning those words Masonic are!
Come, let us contemplate them, they are worthy of a thought,
In the very soul of Masonry those precious words are wrought.

We meet upon the Level, though from every station come,
The rich man from his mansion, and the poor man from his home:
For the one must leave his greatness outside the Mason's door,
While the other finds his level upon the checkered floor.

We part upon the Square, for the world must have its due;
We mingle with the multitude, a faithful band and true,
But the influence of our gatherings in Masonry is green;
And we long upon the Level to renew the happy scene.

There's a world where all are equal; we are hurrying toward it fast:
We shall meet upon the Level there, when the gates of death are pass'd;
We shall stand before the Orient, and our Master will be there,
To try the blocks we offer with his own unerring Square.

We shall meet upon the Level there, but never thence depart;
There's a Mansion—'t is all ready for each trusting, faithful
heart;
There's a Mansion and a welcome, and a multitude is there,
Who have met upon the Level, and been tried upon the Square.

Let us meet upon the Level, then, while laboring patient here;
Let us meet and let us labor, though the labor be severe;
Already in the western sky the signs bid us prepare
To gather up our Working Tools, and part upon the Square.

Hands round, ye faithful Masons, in the bright, fraternal chain;
We part upon the Square below to meet in heaven again;
O what words of precious meaning those words Masonic are—
We meet upon the Level, and we part upon the Square!

The ways of science are beautiful. Knowledge is attained by degrees. Wisdom dwells with contemplation. There are we to seek her. Though the passage be difficult, the further we proceed the easier it will come.

If we are united, our society will flourish. Let all things give place to peace and good fellowship. Uniting in the grand design, let us be happy in ourselves, and endeavor to contribute to the happiness of others. Let us promote the useful arts, and by them mark our superiority and distinction. Let us cultivate the moral virtues, and improve in all that is good and amiable. Let the genius of Masonry preside over our conduct, and under its sovereign sway let us act with becoming dignity. Let our recreations be innocent and pursued with moderation. Never let us expose our character to derision. Thus shall we act in conformity with our precepts, and support the name we have always borne, of being a reputable, a regular, and a uniform society.

The Level.—The pride of birth, talent, and circumstances which so powerfully affect the mind of their possessors forms the most serious obstacle with which the Masonic laborer has to contend. To assist him in a task in which so many fail, the Level is presented to him, and its emblematical meaning expounded. He is admonished that our entrance upon earth, as well as our exit, is humble; that the inclemencies of life equally afflict us; that the baleful passions of human nature know no distinctions of rank; that sorrow, sickness, disease, and mental afflictions are equally distributed; that, in truth, all mankind do "stand upon a Level," so far as their relations to the Author of their being is concerned. These thoughts are calculated to level our pride with the plane on which God has designed us to move. In the burial service of Masonry the reference to the Level is exceedingly appropriate. In the installation ceremonies it is said: "The Level demonstrates that we are descended from the same stock, partake of the same nature, and share the same hope; because a time will come, and the wisest know not how soon, when all distinctions but that of goodness will cease, and Death, the grand leveler of human greatness, reduce us to the same state." The remarks made upon the emblem of "the right angle, horizontal, and perpendicular," upon a preceding page, may be used here.

The qualifications necessary to form a worthy member of our Order are a wise philanthropy, pure morality, inviolable secrecy, and a taste for the polite arts.

I. *Our Philanthropy.*—An ancient maxim was that the whole world is, in effect, a great republic, of which every nation is a family, and every particular person a child. To revive and spread abroad this maxim, drawn from the nature of man, is one of the ends of our establishment. We wish to unite all men of an agreeable humor and enlightened understanding, not only by the love of the polite arts, but still more by the great principles of virtue. From such a union the interests of the Fraternity become the interests of all mankind. From such every nation may draw solid knowledge, and all the subjects of different kingdoms may unite without jealousy, live without disorder, and mutually love one another without renouncing their country. Freemasonry instructs in our duty to the Supreme Architect of the universe, to our neighbors, and to ourselves. It instructs us to be peaceable citizens to the civil powers, and never to be concerned in plots and conspiracies against the well-being of the nations. It teaches truth, peace, and concord. It bids us open our ears to the cries of the unfortunate, and to extend our hands to them with the cup of consolation. It unites men of all nations in one affectionate band of brotherhood. It shows us that we are all upon a level, and that merit is the only just distinction. It orders us to live within compass, and always to act upon the square with the world and with one another. It is not gloomy, but cheerful. It forbids intemperance, but encourages rational mirth and innocent pleasure. In short, it is a superstructure fixed with solid firmness on the broad basis of moral and social virtue.

II. *Our Morality.*—Sound morality is the second disposition required in our society. Let a man's religion or mode of it be what it will, we do not exclude him from the benefits and advantages of our Order, provided he believes in the glorious Architect of heaven and earth, and practices the sacred duties of morality. We are directed to expand our hearts with the most generous sentiments, to root out bigotry, and stop the cruel hand of persecution. We are bid to unite with virtuous men of the most distant countries and opposite opinions; to unite with them in the firm and pleasing bond of fraternal love; to regard them with the truest affection.

As a severe, cruel, gloomy, and unsociable philosophy disgusts men with virtue, we are desirous of rendering it amiable by the allurements of innocent pleasures, agreeable music, pure joy, and rational gayety. Our sentiments are not what the profane world and ignorant vulgar imagine them to be; all the vices of the heart are banished from them, as well as irreligion, libertinism, excess and debauchery.

We banish from our Lodge every dispute which may tend to alter the tranquillity of the mind and gentleness of the manner, or to destroy those sentiments of friendship and that perfect harmony to be found only in the retrenching all indecent excesses and discordant passions.

The obligations that are laid upon us are to protect our brethren by our authority, to enlighten them by our understanding, to edify them by our virtues, to sacrifice every personal resentment toward them, and diligently to seek for every thing that will best contribute to the peace, concord, and credit of our society.

III. *Our Secrecy.*—We have secrets among us. They compose a language sometimes mute and sometimes very eloquent, to be communicated at the greatest distance, and to know our brethren by, let their country or their language be what it may. What has scarcely happened to any other society has happened to us. Our Lodges have been established in and are now spread over all polite nations, and yet among so great a multitude of men, no brother has ever yet betrayed our secrets. Dispositions the most volatile, the most indiscreet, and the least trained up to secrecy, learn this great science as soon as they enter among us. So great an empire over the mind has this idea of brotherly union! This inviolable secrecy powerfully contributes to link together the subjects of different kingdoms, and to facilitate and render mutual between them the communication of benefits. We have many examples in the annals of our Order of brethren traveling into foreign parts, and, finding themselves distressed, have made themselves known to our Lodges and received all needful assistance. We are connected by solemn promises: if any one should fail in the solemn promises that connect us, there is no greater punishment than the remorse of conscience, the infamy of perfidy, and expulsion from our society.

To prevent the abuses that befell the fraternities of Greece and Egypt, women are excluded from our Order. It is not that we do not pay a natural and due regard to that most beauteous part of the creation, or that we are unjust enough to look upon them as incapable of secrecy, but because their presence might insensibly alter the purity of our maxims and our manners. We are afraid that Love would enter with them, and draw us to his flowery, tempting paths, where Jealousy would diffuse his venom through our hearts, and from affectionate brethren transform us into implacable rivals.

IV. *Our Taste for the Polite Arts.*—The fourth qualification necessary to enter into our Order is a taste for useful science and liberal arts of every kind. These improve the heart as much as the understanding. They moderate the selfish affections, sweeten and harmonize the temper, and the better fit men for social happiness, that happiness which Freemasonry most zealously endeavors to promote.

THE PLUMB.—It only needs a glance at a "bowed and tottering wall," or a building inclining sensibly from the perpendicular, or, what is more common and far more painful, a human being of either sex, wandering from the paths of rectitude, to learn the lesson of this emblem. The Plumb-line seems designed by the Author of virtue to teach us what safety there is in truth.

Who wears the Plumb, behold how true
His words and walk! and could we view
The chambers of his soul,
Each thought enshrined, so pure, so good,
By the stern line of rectitude,
Points upward to the goal.

The Plumb admonishes us to walk uprightly in our several stations; to hold the scale of justice in equal poise; to observe the just medium between intemperance and pleasure, and to make our passions and prejudices coincide with the line of our duty. It is the interior of moral rectitude, teaching us to avoid dissimulation in conversation and action, and to direct our paths to the path which leads to immortality. Read here the remarks upon a previous page relative to the emblem of "the right angle, the horizontal, and the perpendicular."

RECEPTION ON THE SQUARE.—As we remarked on a preceding page, under the head "Theory of the Fellow

Craft," this degree is in strictness the working degree of the institution. All its analogies relate to labor and pilgrimage. The Fellow Crafts came from Phœnicia to erect the temples and other stately edifices of Solomon; we engage to erect more stately edifices for our King—"the King of kings and Lord of lords." No effort is spared to impress upon the Fellow Crafts that "they should eat no man's bread for naught;" and among the methods employed is the application of the Square. To try the works of every Mason, the Square is presented as the probation of his life, proving whether his works are regular and uniform or not.

> Who wears the Square upon his breast,
> Does in the sight of God attest,
> And in the face of man,
> That all his actions will compare
> With the Divine, the unerring Square,
> That squares great virtue's plan.

Masons should be of one principle and one rank without the distinctions of pride and pageantry; intimating that from high to low the minds of Masons should be inclined to good works, above which no man stands exalted by his fortune.

THE ATTENTIVE EAR, THE INSTRUCTIVE TONGUE, THE FAITHFUL BREAST.—The use of these three emblems is so natural as scarcely to require comment. Information upon all the inculcations of Masonry is chiefly acquired through the *attentive ear*, both the eye and the hand being subordinate to that. Ignorance is the secret of indolence in Masonry: the idle relish not, because they know not. Though the mine is rich, they have never penetrated to its bed of golden treasures. Strange that any men, too careless to moralize, or too stupid to discern, should enter the porch of Masonry only to fall asleep in the arms of indolence and dullness.

It is a marked truth in the operations of Masonry, that he who has the *instructive tongue* is ever ready to communicate the science to those entitled to receive it. The genius that conducted him through the mystic temple inspired him with all the virtues of the institution. The annals of the Order are full of the names of those whose ready and silvery tongue found no subjects more worthy to be expatiated upon than those connected with Freemasonry.

The third of this splendid trio is the *faithful breast.* Of all societies, this has been the most distinguished for the inviolable secrecy which its members have preserved. Neither the thunders of the Vatican, nor the tortures of the Inquisition, nor the fierce demands of a depraved public opinion, have succeeded in extorting from the *faithful breast* those things so solemnly deposited there.

HOPE.—We have in no author so good a definition of this emblem as that by the Apostle Paul, in his declaration "that by two immutable things, in which it was impossible for God to lie, [referring to his *promise* and his *oath*,] we might have a strong consolation, who have fled for refuge, to lay hold of the hope set before us, which hope we have, as an anchor of the soul, both sure and steadfast, and which entereth into that within the veil." The same eloquent writer in another passage declares: "We are saved by hope; if we hope for that which we see not, then do we with patience wait for it." The Psalmist has declared, "Happy is he whose hope is in the

Lord his God." His son, the wise King, adds: "The righteous hath hope in his death." The Prophet Joel avers "the Lord will be the hope of his people, and the strength of the children of Israel."

As we sit in our respective places in the Lodge, and look upon the open Word in the midst, we may deem that there is a treasury of hopes contained in that book, both for this world and that which is to come. The dealings of God with his ancient people afford a sure foundation that he who is unchangeable in justice, goodness, and mercy, can not fail to render to those who, by patient continuance in well-doing, shall merit his favor, all needed blessings. These are the inculcations of the emblem of Hope.

JACHIN AND BOAZ.—It can not be doubted that the most striking and attractive objects to a person approaching the Temple up Mount Moriah were the brazen Pillars upon the east. Whether to the stranger, who only considered them as architectural ornaments, or to the informed Israelite, who read in their names, dimensions, cavities, and ornaments many of the most useful inculcations in his religious code, these Pillars were the first to catch the eye and the last to fade upon the memory. The height of these transcendent spires is variously given at eighteen and thirty-five cubits: the latter is the more likely, whether we estimate the due proportion between the diameter four cubits, or the magnitude of the great building before which they stood. Nothing less than thirty-five cubits will answer the requirements of the Fellow Craft's lecture, which sets the proportions between the heights and diameters of pillars at seven, eight, nine, ten, and ten for the Tuscan, Doric, Ionic, Corinthian, and Composite Orders respectively. As the particular order of architecture used in these Pillars is not given, we can not designate the exact proportion applicable; but to none of them will a height of eighteen cubits apply.

The names of these grand and awe-inspiring objects are full of meaning to a Freemason. The right Pillar—that is, the one on the south side of the door of entrance—was called "Jachin;" literally, "He will establish." The left Pillar—that is, the one on the north side of the door of entrance—was called "Boaz;" literally, "In it is power." Uniting the two definitions into one, the allusion is to the Divine promise that in strength God would perpetually establish the kingdom of Israel in the family of David. This, in the Masonic system, implies the endurance and strength of our institution, which at the end of its three thousand years of history stands more firmly upon its basis than ever before.

The cavity and ornaments of the Pillars are equally emblematical. Upon the chapiters were nets of checker-work, wreaths of chain-work, seven upon each chapiter, also lily-work, and two hundred pomegranates in rows, upon each. To the instructed Israelite passing between the Pillars, these symbols betokened the great lessons of unity, peace, and plenty, and taught him that the spirit of unity produces peace, and that the combination of unity and peace is divinely blessed to plenty. The globes or pommels upon the chapiters, with their proper scientific teachings, conveyed also the Masonic meaning, expressed upon a previous page, that the charities of Freemasons should be as boundless as the spheres.

THE ANGLE OF 90°.—The application of the right

angle to the center of the earth illustrates the sphere of the Mason's duty and the restraints which he should impose upon the inclinations of his heart, not to wander beyond the angular limits of Masonic propriety. Upon the Angle of 90° the Fellow Craft, metaphorically, is tried, and happy he whose life and conduct shall bear so rigid a test. A very small deviation from this angle, though it may not be perceptible to man, is distinctly so to God, who is our Divine Master, and is to reward us not merely according to the amount of our works, but according to the accuracy with which they adapt themselves to the angle he has traced out for us. It may be that the heathen and the uncultivated denizens of the isles are not prescribed by an Angle so broad as that which is presented to us. God is merciful, and will not place upon any person more responsibilities than he has moral strength to bear; but to us who, in addition to the light of civilization, the Bible and Christianity have the brilliancy of Freemasonry shining within our souls, it is hard to see what excuse we can present our Heavenly Master in the Judgement-day for a deficiency in the angular propriety of our lives. The Angle of 90° is emphatically one of the working tools of our *profession;* let us see that it is not less so of our *practice.*

THE SECOND SECTION.

THE Second Section of the Fellow Craft's Lecture treats of the entrance into the Middle Chamber of the Temple; the objects that attract the candidate's attention there; the duty of a reasonable observance of the Sabbath-day; the numerous and valuable studies recommended to his mind; the rich and ample wages secured him for his labor, and the solemn reverence due from Masons unto the name of God. Properly delivered, this is the most dramatic and beautiful ceremony yet treated upon in this volume. It fully justifies us in claiming for this grade of Masonry that it particularizes circumstances of great importance to the Fraternity, and confirms many of our traditional tenets and customs by sacred and profane record. There is a store of valuable knowledge developed from this lecture, founded on reason, tradition, and the Sacred Record, both entertaining and instructive.

Operative and Speculative Masonry.—The frequent use in this volume of the terms "Operative" and "Speculative" requires an explanation. To the members of this institution was anciently given the erection of all great edifices. The secrets of architecture were then parts of the secrets of Freemasonry, and none could undertake a temple, a palace, or other grand erection, until he had passed the portals of the Masonic Lodge and acquired the scientific knowledge there treasured up. Then Operative and Speculative Masonry were blended; those who built the actual temple also built the moral one. But through the lapse of ages, the secrets of operative architecture have been given out to the world, leaving only the mysteries of the moral building. Speculative Masonry, therefore, contemplates in theory what the operative builder reduces to practice, and the tools of the workmen are only used as emblems in the construction of "the house not made with hands, eternal in the heavens." In this thought the following lines are conceived:

Darkly hid beneath the quarry,
  Masons, many a true block lies;
Hands must shape and hands must carry,
  Ere the stone the Master prize.
    Seek for it, measure it,
    Fashion it, polish it,
  Then the Overseer will prize.

What though shapeless, rough, and heavy,
  Think ye God his work will lose?
Raise the block, the strength he gave ye,
  Fit it for the Master's use.
    Seek for it, measure it,
    Fashion it, polish it,
  Then the Overseer will use.

'T was for this our fathers banded;
  Through life's quarries they did roam,
Faithful-hearted, skillful-handed,
  Bearing many a true block home:
    Noticing, measuring,
    Fashioning, polishing,
  For their glorious Temple-home.

THE SEVENTH DAY OF THE WEEK.—As the Creator of all things has put it on record that he would have his creatures give the seventh day of each week wholly to him and his service, thus commemorating the great fact of the creation, this has been adopted among the landmarks of our institution. It is the oldest of all observances, this day being consecrated in the first division of time after the creation. The Almighty Maker selected it for his own period of refreshment and rest after the completion of his labors, and we in like manner give the hours to bodily rest and the refreshment of the soul. No Lodge may lawfully meet to work upon the Sabbath-day, and no brother give of its sacred time to his ordinary pursuits.

The title given to the Jewish day of rest was "the Sabbath;" it is from a Hebrew word signifying rest. Since the Christian era, the day of rest is called the Lord's Day, because it is now commemorative of Christ's resurrection from the dead; and there is thus connected with it an affectionate remembrance of the whole character and offices of Him to whose service and glory it is to be devoted. Sunday was the name given by the heathens to the first day of the week, because it was the day on which they worshiped the sun, and this name, together with those of the other days of the week, has been continued to our times.

The sanctification of one-seventh portion of time by man is regarded throughout the whole of the Old Testament Scriptures as a fundamental principle of duty, and no sin, except perhaps idolatry, is threatened with heavier penalties than Sabbath-breaking.

The Divine commandment which stands the fourth in the Decalogue, "Remember the Sabbath-day to keep it holy," is founded on the fact that the seventh day was blessed and hallowed by God himself, and that he requires his creatures to keep it holy to him. This commandment is of universal and perpetual obligation. The object to be accomplished by the institution is general, and applies to all people every-where with like force. Wherever there is a human creature capable of contemplating the character of the Supreme Being, of studying his revealed will, and of considering his own immortal destiny, this commandment requires him to consecrate at least one-seventh part of his time to these holy purposes. The terms of the commandment do not fix the precise day in order, except that it is to be *every seventh day*. In other words, it simply requires that after six days of labor, one day is to be given to rest.

There is abundant evidence from history that the seventh day of the week has been observed from the earliest times as a day of rest; and the change from the seventh to the first day does not in any degree change or impair the obligation to sanctify a seventh portion of our time. So far from it, the sacredness and glory of the day are much increased by its association with that great event on which our hope of life and immortality entirely depends.

It seems to be admitted, by intelligent men of every class and profession, that the observance of a weekly day of rest is as essential to our intellectual and physical as to our moral and spiritual nature.

The simple rule as to the mode of observing the day seems to be this: that there should be a cheerful resting all the day from such worldly employments and recreations as may be lawful on other days, and the spending the whole time in the public or private worship of God, except so much as may be occupied by works of necessity or mercy. To test the propriety of any act or pursuit on that day, it is only needful to inquire whether the doing of it will tend to advance us in holy exercises and affection, and in *preparation for the heavenly rest*, or whether it is an act of necessity which can not be postponed without serious injury.

THREE, FIVE, AND SEVEN.—Mystical numbers form important parts in the symbolisms of Freemasonry. The numbers three, five, and seven are the most suggestive of these. Scriptural history shows how frequently they were introduced in sacred events.

"There are three that bear record in heaven: the Father, the Word, and the Holy Ghost, and these three are one." This passage expresses the whole theory of the Masonic trinity. The three principal officers of the Lodge, corresponding with the three original degrees in Masonry, are examples of the uses to which this number is applied.

The number five is not less suggestive in the Masonic rituals. There are five orders in architecture that are recognized among Freemasons: the Tuscan, Doric, Ionic, Corinthian, and Composite, of which the three central ones are most highly esteemed in speculative Masonry. There are five senses in human nature: hearing, seeing, touching, smelling, and tasting, of which the first three are so highly estimated in the Masonic system, that no person who has lost any one of them can lawfully be made a Mason. Among the furniture of the sanctuary and the temple, there were five golden candlesticks on either side of the oracle.

The number seven has even more numerous allusions in the rituals. There are seven liberal arts and sciences inculcated in the Masonic system; viz.: grammar, rhetoric, logic, arithmetic, geometry, music, and astronomy, of which the fifth, generally, is most highly estimated. There are seven days in the week; the seventh year was anciently directed to be a sabbath of rest for all things, and the law was directed to be read to the people. A person was commanded to forgive his offending brother seven times, which our Savior extended to seventy times seven. In the sacrificial service the blood was sprinkled seven times before the altar. Solomon, in his allegory of the house of wisdom, says that it has seven pillars. Seven resurrections are enumerated in Scripture. The series of celestial worlds is said to consist of seven, of which the highest is the most beatific. The book of Revelations, the most symbolical series of writings extant, embodies nearly all its mysteries under the number seven—as seven churches, seven golden candlesticks, seven stars, seven lamps representing the seven spirits, the book with seven seals, the seven kings, seven thunders, the dragon with seven heads and seven crowns, seven angels bringing seven plagues, and seven vials of wrath. In our lectures, perfection is likened to gold seven times purified in the fire.

In the application of these numbers in the Fellow Craft's ritual, lengthy and beautiful discourses upon the Order in architecture and the seven liberal arts and sciences are delivered, which, being found in the Monitor, need no repetition here.

THE EAR OF CORN.—Much may be said of the expressiveness of this emblem, suspended, in all well-arranged Lodges, over the Junior Warden's chair. As the contiguity of a fall of water to a field of standing corn gives vigor to the plant, so the graces of the Divine Spirit give nourishment to the good man's piety, and make it fruitful. The Scriptural light thrown upon this emblem is that in the eleventh chapter of Judges. Fifty-one years after the celebrated exploit of Gideon at the well Harod, the Ammonites came out of their deserts eastward, and invaded Palestine in great numbers. A part of them came up into Gilead and encamped at Aroer. Jephthah, whose residence was at Mizpeh, near by, collected together an army from the surrounding tribes, attacked the Ammonites, achieved a great victory, and rescued twenty cities from their hands which they had taken. By this heroic deed the country was rid of its oppressors. On Jephthah's return home occurred that pathetic tragedy which has made the name of Jephthah's daughter immortal in prose and song.

Shortly afterward the Ephraimites, whose tribe was located on the opposite side of the river westward, taking bitter offense at Jephthah for slighting them in his call for soldiers, or, what is more likely, angry that they were omitted in the distribution of the spoils, crossed the river with a great army and threatened his destruction. Jephthah was in no whit intimidated, but at once recalled his warriors from their homes, and defeated the Ephraimites. Resolved to punish them for their unprovoked assault, he sent portions of his army to the fords in their rear, and intercepting them, slew all who attempted to pass, to the number of forty-two thousand. This was a blow which that haughty tribe never forgot.

As a measure for identifying the Ephraimites at the fords, an *ear of corn* was hung upon a branch and each traveler was requested to give its name. The proper word in Hebrew for an ear of corn is "Shibboleth," so pronounced in the pure language. But the Ephraimites, having a *patois* of their own, were unable thus to express the first syllable. They called it "Sibboleth," just as the Arabs pronounce the same word to the present day. Their defect of utterance was fatal to them, for every man who thus named the *ear of corn* was summarily dispatched.

In relation to this singular transaction, which in the

rituals of the Fellow Craft plays a prominent part, a celebrated English writer of the last century says: "The application which is made of certain words among Masons is as a testimony of their retaining their original one uninfringed, and their first faith with the brotherhood uncorrupted. And to render their words and phrases more abstruse and secure, they selected such as by acceptation in the Scriptures or otherwise might puzzle the ignorant by a double implication. Thus, 'Shibboleth,' should we have adopted the Eleusonian mysteries, would answer as an avowal of our profession, the word implying 'ears of corn.' But taking its derivative from the Greek tongue, it is equivalent to 'Colo lapidem,' implying that we retain and keep inviolate our obligations as the 'Jurimentum per jovem lapidem,' the most obligatory oath held among the heathens."

THE LETTER G.—A brother entering the Lodge while at work, has his attention turned first to the emblems upon the Altar, of which one is the immortal Word of God, and next to an object suspended over the Master's Chair, *an emblem of the letter G*. This is the initial letter of the name of Deity, that Being before whom Masons of every degree bow and adore. The full bearing of this emblem is conveyed in the following lines:

That Name! I heard it at my mother's knee,
  When looking up, the dear, remembered face
Beaming on mine, so fond, so tenderly,
  She prayed that GOD her little son would bless.

That Name! I spoke it when I entered here,
  And bowed the knee, as man in worship must;
From my heart's center, with sincerity,
  I cried aloud, "In GOD is all my trust."

That Name! I saw it o'er the Master's chair,
The "Hieroglyphic bright," and bending low,
Paid solemn homage to the symbol there
That speaks of God, before whom all should bow.

That Name! I whispered at the Altar here,
When dangers thickened, and when death was nigh;
In solemn silence, and with soul sincere,
I prayed, "O God be with me, if I die!"

That Name! the last upon my faltering tongue,
Ere death shall seal it, it shall surely be;
The pass-word to the bright, angelic throng,
Whose God is God to all eternity.

That Name then, brothers, ever gently speak,
Above all father's, mother's name, revered;
What bounties from His gracious hand we take!
O, be His honor to our souls endeared.

Corn, Wine, and Oil.—The bounties of our Heavenly Father have supplied us, while we sojourn below, with all necessary comforts of food, shelter, and clothing. The earth abundantly yields them to the industrious laborer; from our mother's breast we pass to the yielding sources of the soil. The emblem of *corn*, implying all the nutritious fruits of the earth; the emblem of *wine*, implying all that nature affords to gladden the heart, and the emblem of *oil*, which to Oriental nations is quite as important as the others, represent nature's bounties, the wages of practical labor. King Solomon stipulated to pay the Temple-builders, for their service, "twenty thousand measures of beaten wheat and twenty thousand measures of barley, and twenty thousand baths of wine and twenty thousand baths of oil." Thus bountifully did that large-hearted monarch provide for those who should do him service in his erections for God. Shall we not have as bountiful returns for our labor? Toiling in the nobler system of architecture, the building up of the human soul, and laboring under the supervision of the Supreme Architect of the Universe, let us not doubt the liberality of our Master or the certainty of ample reward. Plenty, health, and peace wait upon them that do the works of God.

THE PERFECT ASHLARS.—The spirit of this whole section is conveyed in the following lines:

The sunbeams from the eastern sky
  Flash from yon blocks exalted high,
And on their polished fronts proclaim
  The framer and the builder's fame.

Glowing beneath the fervid noon,
  Yon marble dares the southern sun;
Yet tells that wall of fervid flame,
  The framer and the builder's fame.

The chastened sun adown the west,
  Speaks the same voice and sinks to rest;
No sad defect, no flaw to shame
  The framer and the builder's fame.

Beneath the dewy night, the sky
  Lights up ten thousand lamps on high;
Ten thousand lamps unite to name
  The framer and the builder's fame.

Perfect in line, exact in square,
  These Ashlars of the Craftsmen are;
They will to coming time proclaim
  The framer and the builder's fame.

The best specimen of a Perfect Ashlar presented in the Masonic ranks, in this country, is George Washington. He was indeed a paragon in Freemasonry, an exemplar of its virtues and its graces. There is no degree of moral improvement suggested by Masonic teachings to which he did not *aspire*, and few to which he had not *attained*. His life as a citizen, a statesman, and a patriot, the world has by heart; his career as a Freemason is not less worthy of admiration and respect. In the pressure of a long and doubtful war, when his faculties were concentrated in the never-ceasing details of command, he was ever ready to turn his thoughts to the claims of a distressed, worthy brother, prompt to attend Lodge meetings, happy to respond to Masonic courtesies.

The bust or portrait of Washington should be placed conspicuously in every Lodge-room. Not only should we become familiar with those majestic features at our dwellings, but, in conjunction with the emblems of the Lodge, they should appear the brightest and most significant emblem of them all.

THE MASTER MASON.

O DEATH, thy hand is weighty on the breast
  Of him who lies within thy grasp!
No power can raise the captive from his rest
  Whom thy strong hand doth clasp.

The tears of broken hearts do fall in vain:
  Their sighs are wasted o'er the grave;
Thou laugh'st to scorn the solemn funeral strain,
  For there is none to save.

From age to age, mankind hath owned thy sway—
  Submissive bowed beneath thy hand;
The hoary head, the infant of a day,
  The loveliest of the band.

And thou hast struck the true and faithful now,
  The model of Masonic faith;
It was a cruel and a dastard blow,
  O stern, unyielding death!

Yet, boastful monster, ye shall have release,
  Thy weighty hand, relentless power,
Shall be withdrawn, and all thy mockings cease,
  And all thy triumphs o'er.

The Lion of the Tribe of Judah comes—
  See in the heavenly east the sign!
To rend the sepulchers, disclose the tombs,
  And place thee, monster, in!

THE MASTER MASON.

THE FIRST SECTION.

THE THEORY OF THE DEGREE OF MASTER MASON.

THE Degree of Master Mason is suggestive of government over men. The Apprentice and the Fellow Craft draw the materials from quarry and forest, shape them, remove them to the places designed for them, and raise them to the wall: this is physical labor. All this requires a designing head, a draughtsman, and a superintendent, and this is the Master Mason. The same necessity exists in Speculative or Moral Masonry.

To the Master Mason were intrusted the secrets of architecture, plans, measurements, and estimates, the weight, tenacity, and durability of materials, and all that learning needful to transform rude stones and the trunks of trees into edifices that should be the wonder and delight of the earth. With such transcendent privileges there was coupled a heavy burden of covenants, and he was expected to exemplify before his fellow-laborers every virtue and grace symbolized on the Trestle-Board of the Master Builder.

A late writer has elegantly said: We have seen the type of man complete in moral worth and intellectual culture. What more is left? Communion with his Maker. The mere knowledge of Deity is that of our august Creator, whom we are to reverence and in whom alone we are to put our trust. But we have not yet seen Him walking upon the earth and holding open communion with the sons of men. Man has not been ennobled by personal contact with the All-Holy. Let us suppose three brethren, types respectively of moral, intellectual, and physical perfection, joined together in holy fellowship, which should make their very souls as one, might they not in mystic union call upon the great and sacred name of Deity and receive an answer to their prayer? That such an idea did prevail, we have sufficient proof, and it is to this, rather than to any mere utilitarian views, that we are to look for the rule which, in a purely speculative institution, so sternly demands physical as well as moral and intellectual integrity.

The Degree of Master Mason is a type of the communion of man with God. Long before the incarnation of that great Being was the hope entertained of seeing Him with mortal eyes, and no exertions were deemed too great to insure that consummation. With us these ideas are but a type, for we have that realization so longed for by the brethren of old. And yet, as a type, how interesting it is to look back upon their struggles to look forward into what is now so bright and clear!

We now find man complete in morality and intelligence, with the story of religion added, to insure him of the protection of the Deity, and guard him against ever going astray. These three degrees thus form a perfect and harmonious whole.

THE COMPASS.—The use of the Compass, whose beautiful allegory was explained in a preceding grade, is peculiarly adapted to the present Degree. Within its extreme points, when properly extended, are found the grand principles of Friendship, Morality, and Brotherly Love. No subject can more properly engage the attention than the humane and generous feelings planted by nature in the human breast. Friendship is traced through the circle of private connections to the grand system of universal philanthropy, but the Brotherly Love so well known to the Masonic family is one of the purest emanations of earthly friendship. A community of sentiment and feeling creates a community of interest, cultivated and cherished by every brother.

Morality is practical virtue, of which so much is said in the preceding degrees. It is the journey of Wisdom, pursuing and disseminating happiness. It is no cold speculation, but a living principle. Saint John, himself one of the purest exemplars of these three virtues, has left it on record, that if a man say, I love God, and hateth his brother, *he is a liar;* for he that loveth not his brother, whom he hath seen, how *can he love God*, whom he hath not seen? Beloved, if God so loved us, we ought also to love one another; and this commandment have we from Him, That he who loveth God, love *his brother also.* So sings the Masonic lyrist:

By one God created, by one Savior saved,
By one Spirit lighted, with one mark engraved,
We learn through the wisdom our spirits approve,
To cherish the spirit of Brotherly Love.

In the land of the stranger we Masons abide,
In forest, in quarry, on Lebanon's side;
Yon Temple we build it, its plan 's from above,
And we labor supported by Brotherly Love.

Though the service be hard, and the wages be scant,
If the Master accept it, our hearts are content;
The prize that we toil for, we 'll have it *above*,
When the Temple's completed, in Brotherly Love.

Yes, yes, though the week may be long, it will end;
Though the Temple be lofty, the key-stone will stand;
And the Sabbath, blest day, every thought will remove,
Save the memory fraternal of Brotherly Love.

THE ALTAR.—The sacrifices made upon the Masonic Altar are the bloodless offerings of the soul. David describes them when he says, "The sacrifices of God are a broken spirit; a broken and a contrite heart, O God, thou wilt not despise." These may be individualized as sacrifices of our own will, of feelings of contempt, anger, and hatred; of tale-bearing and indiscretion; of selfishness and the indulgence of our passions. Such are the offerings made upon the open Law and in front of the emblem of the letter G.

Friendship, on wing etherial flying round,
Stretches her arm to bless the hallowed ground;
Humanity, well pleased, here takes her stand,
Holding her daughter, Pity, by the hand;
Here Charity, which soothed the widow's sigh,
And wipes the dew-drop from the orphan's eye;
Here stands Benevolence, whose large embrace
Uncircumscribed takes in the human race;
She sees each narrow tie, each private end,
Indignant, Virtue's universal friend;
Scorning each frantic zealot, bigot tool,
She stamps on Masons' breasts her Golden Rule.

THE TROWEL.—The Master Mason is not restricted to a single implement, or set of implements, for his mystic work; but the most appropriate tool in his department is the Trowel—the emblem of peace—used to spread the cement of brotherly love and affection; that cement which unites us into one sacred band or society of friends and brothers, amongst whom no contention should ever exist save that noble contention, or rather emulation, of who best can work and best agree. The parts of a building can not be united without proper cement; no more can the social compact be maintained without the binding influence of love.

CHARITY.—So much has been said in other pages of this volume upon Charity, or more properly Love, that it would be superfluous to enlarge further upon this subject. No one has so clearly defined it as the Apostle who so thoroughly experienced it, the Evangelist John. His soul was filled with this divine emanation when he wrote, "He that loveth his brother abideth in the light, and there is none occasion of stumbling in him." "We know that we have passed from death unto life, because we love the brethren." "Let us not love in word, neither in tongue, but in deed and truth." "Brethren, let us love one another, for love is of God, and every one that loveth is born of God and honoreth God. He that loveth not, honoreth not God, for God is love." "Brethren, if God so loved us, we ought also to love one another."

Under the term "Charity," the Apostle Paul, in a masterly summing-up of the subject, writes: "Though I speak with the tongues of men and of angels, and though I have the gift of prophesy, and understand all mysteries and all knowledge, and though I bestow all my goods to feed the poor, and though I give my body to be burned, and have not charity, it profiteth me nothing. And now abideth Faith, Hope, Charity, these three; but the greatest of these is Charity."

PRAYER.—The posture of bended knees is often alluded to in Scripture. Solomon kneeled down upon his knees before the congregation of Israel, and spread forth his hands toward heaven. Ezra says, "I fell on my knees, and spread out my hands unto the Lord my God." Daniel kneeled on his knees three times a day and prayed. Paul says, "I bow my knees unto the Father."

As an appropriate form of Lodge prayer, in which Masons of all persuasions can unite without compromise of religious principle, the one entitled the Lord's Prayer is the most perfect: "Our Father which art in heaven, hallowed be thy name. Thy kingdom come. Thy will be done in earth, as it is in heaven. Give us this day our daily bread. And forgive us our debts, as we forgive our debtors. And lead us not into temptation, but deliver us from evil. For thine is the kingdom, and the power, and the glory, forever. Amen."

THE FOUNDATION-STONE.

When the Spirit came to Jephthah,
  Animating his great heart,
He arose, put on his armor,
  Girt his loins about to part;
Bowed the knee, implored a blessing,
  Gave an earnest of his faith,
Then, divinely-strung, departed,
  Set for victory or death.

If a rude, uncultured soldier
  Thus drew wisdom from above,
How should we, enlightened laborers,
  Children of the Sire of Love—
How should we, who know "the wisdom,
  Gentle, pure, and peaceable,"
Make a prayerful preparation,
  That our work be square and full!

Lo, the future! One can read it!
  He its darkest chance can bend.
Lo, our wants! how great, how many!
  He abundant means can lend.
Raise your hearts, then, laborers, boldly,
  Build and journey in his trust;
Square your deeds by precepts holy,
  And the end is surely blest.

Vainly will the Builders labor
  If the Overseer is gone;
Vainly gate and wall are guarded
  If the All-seeing is withdrawn:
Only is successful ending
  When the work's begun with care;
Lay your blocks, then, laborers, strongly,
  On the Eternal Rock of Prayer!

THE SECOND SECTION.

THE Second Section is devoted to that combination of duties implied under the figure of "The Five Points of Fellowship;" likewise to the most expressive arrangement of Masonic emblems, "The Broken Column." These two subjects, inserted in the the center of the Master's lecture, form in truth the very heart of the matter, and no Mason can be esteemed well instructed who does not familiarize himself with them. This section recites the historical tradition of the Order, and presents to view a picture of great moral sublimity. It recites the legend, the symbolical interpretation of which testifies our faith in the resurrection of the body and the immortality of the soul; while it also exemplifies an instance of integrity and firmness seldom equaled, and never surpassed.

THE FIVE POINTS OF FELLOWSHIP.—The old records succinctly declare that the Master Mason should not withdraw his hand from a sinking brother; that his foot should never halt in the pursuit of duty; that his prayers should unceasingly ascend for the distressed; that his faithful heart should equally conceal the secrets and the faults of a brother; and that approaching evil should be averted by a friendly admonition. The same thought is more elaborately conveyed in the following, from an author of the last generation:

I. When the necessities of a brother call for my aid and support, I will be ever ready to lend him such assistance, to save him from sinking, as may not be detrimental to myself or connection, if I find him worthy thereof.

II. Indolence shall not cause my footsteps to halt nor wrath turn them aside; but, forgetting every selfish consideration, I will be swift of foot to serve, help, and execute benevolence to a fellow-creature in distress, and more particularly to a brother Mason.

III. When I offer up my ejaculations to Almighty God, I will remember a brother's welfare as my own; for as the voice of babes and sucklings ascends to the Throne of Grace, so most assuredly will the breathings of a fervent heart arise to the mansions of bliss, as our prayers are certainly required of one another.

IV. A brother's secrets, delivered to me as such, I will keep as I would my own; as betraying that trust might be doing him the greatest injury he could sustain in this mortal life. Nay, it would be like the villainy of an assassin who lurks in darkness to stab his adversary when unarmed and least prepared to meet an enemy.

V. A brother's character I will support in his absence as I would in his presence. I will not wrongfully revile him myself, nor will I suffer it to be done by others, if in my power to prevent it. Thus by the Five Points of Fellowship are we linked together in an indivisible chain of sincere affection, brotherly love, relief, and truth.

Another and even more beautiful comment upon the Five Points of Fellowship is the following:

I. When the calamities of our brother call for our aid, we should not withdraw the hand that might sustain him from sinking, but should render him those services which, while they do not encumber or injure our families or fortunes, charity and religion may dictate for the saving of our fellow-creature.

II. From which purpose indolence should not persuade the foot to halt, or wrath turn our steps out of the way; but, forgetting injuries and selfish feelings, and remembering that man was born for the aid of his generation and not for his own enjoyments only, but to do that which is good, we should be swift to have mercy, to save, to strengthen, and execute benevolence.

III. As the good things of this life are partially dispensed, and some persons are opulent while others are in distress, such principles always enjoin a Mason, be he ever so poor, to testify his good-will toward his brother.

Riches alone do not allow the means of doing good. Virtue and benevolence are not confined to the walls of opulence. The rich man from his many talents is required to make extensive works, under the principles of virtue. And yet poverty is no excuse for an omission of that exercise; for, as the cry of innocence ascendeth up to heaven, as the voice of babes and sucklings reaches the throne of God, and as the breathings of a contrite heart are heard in heaven, so a Mason's prayers for the welfare of his brother are required of him.

IV. The fourth principle is, never to injure the confidence of your brother by revealing his secrets, for perhaps that were to rob him of the guard that protects his property or his life. The tongue of a Mason should be without guile and void of offense, speaking truth with discretion, and keeping itself within the rule of judgment, maintaining a heart free of uncharitableness, locking up secrets, and communing in charity and love.

V. As much is required of a Mason in the way of gifts as discretion may limit. Charity begins at home, but, like a fruitful olive-tree planted by the side of a fountain whose boughs overshoot the wall, so is charity. It spreads its arms abroad from the strength and opulence of its station, and lendeth its shade for the repose and relief of those who are gathered under its branches. Charity, when given with imprudence, is no longer a virtue; but when flowing from abundance, it is glorious as the beams of morning, in whose beauty thousands rejoice. When donations extorted by piety are detrimental to a man's family, they become sacrifices to superstition, and, like incense to idols, are disapproved by Heaven.

THE BROKEN COLUMN.—The Broken Column supporting the volume of Divine inspiration; a virgin, of matchless beauty, weeping, supporting in her left hand a funeral urn, commemorative of the departed, and in her right hand a sprig of evergreen; Time, the great leveler and restorer, entwining her disheveled locks in his fingers—this is the array of symbols now presented to the admiring eyes of the candidate. They are calculated to awaken every sentiment of respect, veneration, and fraternal tenderness on the one hand, and on the other to remind us, that although time may lay all earthly grandeur in ruins and deface the loveliness of all terrestrial beauty, yet there is imperishable grandeur joined to unfading beauty and eternal happiness in the world beyond the grave.

'T is done—the dark decree is said,
  That called our friend away;
Submissive bow the sorrowing head,
  And bend the lowly knee.
We will not ask why God has broke
  Our Pillar from its stone,
But humbly yield us to the stroke,
  And say "His will be done."

At last the weary head has sought
  In earth its long repose;
And weeping freres have hither brought
  Their chieftain to his close.
We held his hand, we filled his heart,
  While heart and hand could move,
Nor will we from his grave depart
  But with the rites of love.

This grave shall be a garner, where
  We'll heap our golden corn;

And here, in heart, we 'll oft repair,
  To think of him that's gone;
To speak of all he did and said,
  That 's wise, and good, and pure,
And covenant o'er the hopeful dead,
  In vows that will endure.

O Brother, bright and loving frere,
  O spirit free and pure,
Breathe us one gush of spirit air,
  From off the Heavenly shore;
And say, when these hard toils are done,
  And the Grand Master calls,
Is there for every weary one
  Place in the heavenly halls!

The Unfinished Temple.—The Temple of Masonry is ever in course of construction, ever unfinished. Into its walls successive generations of the wise and good are built; and while time lasts, and the end of all things is delayed, the moral structure is incomplete. But we need not fear its walls will crumble, or that the work will ever cease. The other societies of this world, empires, kingdoms, and commonwealths, being of less perfect constitutions, have been of less permanent duration. Although men have busied themselves through all ages in forming and reforming them, in casting down and building up, yet still their labors have been vain. The reason was—hear it and be wise, ye builders of the present day!—*they daubed with untempered mortar*; they admitted into their structures the base, discordant, heterogeneous materials of pride, ambition, selfishness, malice, guile, hypocrisies, envious and evil speaking, which Freemasonry rejects. Hence their fabrics, unable to support themselves, tumbled to the foundation through inherent weakness, or were shaken to pieces by external violence.

The Egyptian, the Babylonian, the Assyrian, the Persian Empires, the commonwealths of Athens, Sparta, and Rome, with many more of later date, where are they now? "Fallen, fallen, fallen," the weeping voice of history replies. The meteors of our age, the gaze of the world, they rose, they blazed awhile on high, they burst and sunk beneath the horizon, to that place of oblivion where the pale ghosts of departed grandeur fly about in sad lamentations for their former glory.

Such have been the changes and revolutions which, as a Fraternity, we have seen. From the bosom of the Lodge, seated upon an eminence, its foundations reaching the center and its summits the sky, we have beheld, as upon a turbulent ocean at an immense distance beneath us, the states of this world alternately mounted up and cast down, as they have regarded or neglected the principles described above, while, supported by them, the sublime fabric of our constitution has remained unshaken through ages. And thus supported it *shall remain* while the sun opens the day to gild its cloud-capped towers, or the moon leads in the night to checker its starry canopy. The current of things may roll along its basis, the tide of chance and time may beat against its walls, the stormy gusts of malice may assault its lofty battlements, and the heavy rains of calumny may descend upon its spacious roof, but all in vain. A building thus constructed and supported is impregnable from without, and can then only be dissolved when the pillars of the universe shall be shaken, and "the great globe itself, yea, all which we inherit, shall, like the baseless fabric of a vision," pass away at the fiat of the Master Architect.

MONODY OF THE GRAND MASTER.

Dead! and where now those earnest, loving eyes,
Which kindled in so many eyes the light?
Have they departed from our earthly skies,
And left no rays to illuminate the night?

Dead! and where now that hand of sympathy
That welled, and yearned, and with true love o'erflowed?
O heart of love, is the rich treasure dry?
Forever sealed what once such gifts bestowed?

Dead! and where now that generous, nervous hand,
That thrilled each nerve within its generous clasp?
Will it no more enlink the Mystic band,
Hallowing and strengthening all within its grasp?

Heart, eyes, and hand to dust are all consigned;
It was his lot, for he was born of earth:
But the rich treasures of his Master-mind
Abide in heaven, for there they had their birth.

Abide in heaven! O, the enkindling trust!
The record of his deeds remaineth here:
The Acacia blooms beside his silent dust,
And points unerringly the brighter sphere.

Then, though the Shattered Column mark his fate,
And Weeping Virgin weep the Unfinished Fane,
Not altogether are we desolate:
For O, beloved Friend, we meet again!

THE THIRD SECTION.

THIS Section is chiefly devoted to the explanation of the hieroglyphical emblems peculiar to this Degree. As usually given, it presents many useful particulars relative to King Solomon's Temple, a portion of which, in the present volume, are, for convenience sake, transferred to other pages. In the richness of its imagery, this Section resembles the Third Section of the Degree of Entered Apprentice.

WISDOM, STRENGTH, AND BEAUTY.—The emblem of the three Pillars in this section alludes to the three immortal artists who contrived, strengthened, and adorned the sacred Fane. Solomon, King of Israel, first in wisdom, in wealth, in favor with God and man, stands as the Pillar of Wisdom. "His wisdom excelled," says the inspired historian, "the wisdom of all the children of the east country and all the wisdom of Egypt. For he was wiser than all men; than Ethan the Ezrahite, and Heman and Chalcor and Darda, the sons of Mahal. He spoke three thousand proverbs, and his songs were a thousand and five, and he spoke of trees from the cedar tree, that is in Lebanon, even unto the hyssop that springeth out of the wall; he spoke also of beasts and of fowls and of creeping things and of fishes." This is all summed up in this passage: "God gave Solomon wisdom and understanding exceeding much, and largeness of heart even as the sand that is upon the seashore." This was our Pillar of Wisdom.

Our Pillar of Strength was Hiram, King of Phœnicia, a nation of architects and mariners, whose furnishing of skillful builders and choice materials gave to King Solomon all the support necessary for his undertaking.

Our Pillar of Beauty was Hiram Abiff, whose singular proficiency in all the works of the goldsmith, the brass-founder, the dyer and weaver, the lapidary and the jeweler, gave the desired impetus to the adorning of the edifice.

THE COLUMNS AND PILASTERS.—Our monitorial instructor gives the due number of these outward parts of the edifice, by which the visitor from foreign nations, who was not permitted to approach the Temple nearer than the outer courts, could form an idea of the magnitude and splendor of the interior. Of columns proper there were 1,453; of pilasters, 2,906. Upon other pages of this volume a description of the porch and the courts is given, from which we deduce the necessity of so many columns and pilasters in the building.

In the same connection, the lectures of the Master's Degree compute the numbers of the workmen as follows: Grand Masters, 3; Masters, or overseers of the work, 3,300; Fellow Crafts, 80,000; Entered Apprentices, or bearers of burdens, 70,000. These were all classed and arranged by the wisdom of Solomon, that neither envy, discord, nor confusion were suffered to interrupt that universal peace and tranquillity which pervaded the world at this important period. The materials that made up this band were the virtuous and laborious; its master-builders the Enochs, the Noahs, the Abrahams, the Moses, the Joshuas of the age. There was not a signal connected with it which did not point either to man's extremity or to God's opportunity; not a grip which did not speak of human relations demanding human sympathies; not a word that did not tell of power, permanency, or wisdom as the result of active, thorough devotion;

not a ceremony which was not full of instruction upon the great divisions of human knowledge.

LODGE COMBINATIONS.—The number of members essential to the legal opening and working of a Lodge of Entered Apprentices is seven or more, of whom one at least must be a Master Mason.

Where two or three assemble round
  In work the Lord approves,
His spirit with the grasp is found,
  For 'tis the place he loves:
Be now all hearts to friendship given,
For we, the Sons of Light, are *seven*.

The number of members essential to the legal opening and working of a Lodge of Fellow Crafts is five or more, of whom, at least, two must be Master Masons, the other three being Fellow Crafts.

This Lodge of *Five* from Tyre came,
Their leader one of matchless fame;
All through the toiling seasons seven,
Their time upon this work was given.

The number of members essential to the legal opening and working of a Lodge of Master Masons is three or more, all of that Degree. A Lodge attempting to operate in violation of these landmarks, breaks the unity of the sacred numbers three, five, and seven; the Master who permits it violates in an especial manner his own covenants, and the Lodge so offending forfeits the Charter or Warrant under which it works, and which in itself embodies an injunction to adhere to the ancient landmarks.

THE THREE STEPS.—This is an emblem recalling the

various illustrations of the number Three, and this additional one, that human life has three principal stages—youth, manhood, and old age. The first is symbolical of the Entered Apprentice, as suggested under the head of "Theory of the First Degree," on a preceding page. Masons of that grade are therefore exhorted industriously to occupy their minds in the attainment of useful knowledge. The second step is beautifully emblematical of the Fellow Craft, who is exhorted in the lectures of his Degree to apply the knowledge which he acquired as an Entered Apprentice to the discharge of his respective duties to God, his neighbor, and himself. The third step is emblematical of the Master Mason, who, in the enjoyment of those happy reflections consequent upon a well-spent life, prepares his mind for a blissful hereafter.

Corresponding with this emblem the being of man has three periods—time, death, and eternity. Upon one of these steps every member of our widely-spread Order is now standing. He who writes this and he who reads it stands upon the first; but who can anticipate the period of his stay? Upon the second hundreds are standing, gasping, tottering, perhaps dreading the illimitable profound that opens before them, while in the unknown existence of the third is the great mass of those who, like ourselves, have

"Met upon the Level, to part upon the Square."

The Pot of Incense.—This is an emblem of a pure heart, and as such is peculiarly expressive. There is a state of perfection at which the good man may arrive by the influence of vital religion, and such is typified by this emblem. A pure heart perpetually ascends in perfumes of gratitude, like the cloud of celestial white that filled the Temple, and like the heaven-descended flame that burned day and night within the *sanctum sanctorum*. Such is the offering of prayer, the most acceptable incense the human heart can raise.

Incense for the service of the Sanctuary was ordered to be made of frankincense and other gums and spices, the materials and manufacture of which are particularly described in the Divine Law. It was the business of the priest to offer it up, morning and evening, upon an altar especially erected for this purpose, and this was called the Altar of Incense. The preparation of it for common use was positively forbidden; neither could any other composition be offered as incense upon this altar, nor could this be offered by any but the priest. The Incense approved by God under the present dispensation is more fragrant, more costly, and more acceptable than the richest gums of Arabia. The service and the time of offering is in the option of every man. Whenever a Freemason looks upon the emblem, he should be reminded to make at least one ejaculation of thanksgiving, praise, or confession to Him who ever heareth.

The Bee-Hive.—This emblem of industry has peculiar meaning to the members of a society based upon a working model. The slothful inactivity of the rational drone is severely reproved by it. The industrious bee rises early to the labors of the summer day, gathering from the variegated carpet of nature an ample supply of food for the winter of his year. Man, in imitation of this example, might enjoy all the necessaries and even the luxuries of life, while he would avoid vice and temptation and merit the respect of mankind. On the contrary, idleness is the parent of poverty and immorality. Such are the lessons taught by all the working tools—the Gauge and Gavel, the Square, Level and Plumb, and the Trowel—of the Craft. Every day of the six properly devoted to labor should be so divided that while a share may be given to works of charity and devotion, and a share to refreshment and sleep, one measured part may be given to the avocations of life, those callings upon which the interests of society depend.

The proverbs of the wise king abound in rebukes upon indolence and admonition to industry: "Go to the ant, thou sluggard: consider her ways and be wise; which provided her meat in the summer and gathereth her food in the harvest. How long wilt thou sleep, O sluggard? Yet a little sleep, a little slumber, a little folding of the hands to sleep: so shall thy poverty come as one that traveleth, and thy want as an armed man."

The Book of Constitutions guarded by the Tyler's Sword.—So much has been said in this volume upon the importance of secrecy as a Masonic virtue, that the application of this emblem will be easy. The Book of Constitutions, as an emblem, represents all the instruction, esoteric and exoteric, connected with the Masonic ritual. The Tyler of the Lodge, whose emblem, badge, and implement are the Sword, is the guardian of those assemblages held for the purpose of lawfully communicating the secrets of Masonry. Thus the Sword guarding the Book recalls to the memory of the initiate all the instructions communicated to him upon this subject. This emblem will convince the Mason of the policy of preserving inviolably the important secrets which are committed to his breast.

Various passages from the Holy Scriptures are appended to enforce these lessons: "Be ye afraid of the sword, for wrath bringeth the punishments of the sword that ye may know there is a judgment." "Even a fool when he holdeth his peace is counted wise, and he that shutteth his lips is esteemed a man of understanding." "Whoso keepeth his mouth and his tongue, keepeth his soul from troubles. As he that bindeth a stone in a sling, so is he that giveth honor to a fool." "Discretion shall preserve thee, understanding shall keep thee." It will be observed, however, that with us the Sword is but a symbol. There is no punishment in Masonry for the highest crimes, beyond expulsion from the Order.

THE SWORD POINTING TO THE NAKED HEART.—This emblem is the complement of the last. The punishments of Masonry, at the greatest, are but exclusion from the Order. But although Mercy delays the descending stroke of Justice, there is a day appointed in which Justice will be amply avenged, unless Mercy shall secure us in the ark of her retreat. The sword of Almighty vengeance is drawn to reward iniquity, and pointed steadily toward the sinful heart. Were it not for this belief in retributive justice, how painful would be our observations of human life! All history is full of instances of the tyranny of the strong over the weak. How much sin against God and humanity is done privily, of which there is no disclosure in this life! Yet there is a righteous God, and He does not look upon these things without abhorrence. His Law declares: "The ungodly shall not stand in the judgment, nor sinners in the congregation of the righteous." "If I speak of strength, lo, he is strong; and if of judgment, who shall set me a time to plead? for he is not a man as I am, that I should consider him. I will say unto God, do not condemn me."

These are the lessons taught by this emblem. As surely as Masonry encourages us to hope for a reward to the righteous in the world to come, so certainly does it inculcate the doctrine that there is a punishment there for the evil-doer.

THE ALL-SEEING EYE.—This emblem implies that all the ways of man are before the eyes of the Lord, and he pondereth all his goings; that the eyes of the Lord are in every place beholding the evil and the good, and especially upon them that fear him and hope in his mercy.

There is an Eye through blackest night
  A vigil ever keeps;
A vision of unerring light
O'er lowly vale and giddy height—
  The Eye that never sleeps.

Midst poverty and sickness lain
  The lowly sufferer weeps;
What marks the face convulsed with pain?
What marks the softened look again?
  The Eye that never sleeps.

Above the far meridian sun,
  Below profoundest deeps,
Where dewy day his course begun,
Where scarlet marks his labor done—
  The Eye that never sleeps.

No limit bounds the Eternal sight,
  No misty cloud o'ersweeps;
The depths of hell confess the light,
Eternity itself is bright—
  The Eye that never sleeps.

Then rest we calm, though round our head
  The life-storm fiercely sweeps;
What fear is in the blast? What dread
To us has death? an Eye's o'erhead—
  The Eye that never sleeps.

THE ANCHOR AND THE ARK.—Under the emblem of Hope, on a previous page, we explained the manner in which this first of the three theological virtues is inculcated to Freemasons. The Ark, an emblem of that which survived the flood, reminds us of that ark of safety which will waft us securely over this sea of troubles; and when arrived in a celestial harbor, the anchor of a well-grounded hope will moor us forever to that peaceful shore "where the wicked cease from troubling and the weary are at rest." This grace is equally important and pleasing in this world of uncertainty and change. The present moment is sure to possess some ingredient to embitter the chalice of mortal enjoyment, and how effectually are we relieved by the soothing hope that the deficiencies of the present day shall be supplied by to-morrow! The Anchor, which is connected with this emblem, is an emblem of security. When the visions of hope are real and rational, as when we hope in the promises of God, in a future state of happiness to the good, and the like, her anchor is sure and steadfast in the harbor of a celestial country. To this country hope points as the future residence of the virtuous and the good; thither all good Masons hope to arrive.

Green, but far greener is the Faith
That gives us victory over death;
Fragrant, more fragrant far the Hope
That buoys our dying spirits up;
Enduring, but the Charity
That Masons teach will never die.

THE FORTY-SEVENTH PROBLEM.—The history of this problem is much confused; some writers attributing its discovery to one person, some to another. Even the period of its discovery is doubtful; but so many of the most practical operations of architecture and surveying depend upon it, that it is difficult to believe its discovery bears date later than the erection of the Egyptian pyramids. Its adoption into Freemasonry implies that the members of this Order should be lovers of the arts and sciences.

THE HOUR-GLASS.

LIFE'S sands are dropping, dropping,
Each grain a moment dies,
No stay has time, no stopping;
Behold, how swift he flies!
He bears away our rarest,
They smile and disappear,
The cold grave wraps our fairest;
Each falling grain 's a tear.

Life's sands are softly falling,
Death's foot is light as snow;
'T is fearful, 't is appalling
To see how swift they flow:

To read the fatal warning
  The sands so plainly tell
To feel *there's no returning*
  From death's dark shadowy dale.

Life's sands give admonition
  To use its moments well;
Each grain bears holy mission,
  And this the tale they tell:
"Let zeal than time run faster,
  Each grain some good afford,
Then at the last the Master
  Shall double our reward."

THE SCYTHE.—This emblem is trite: as the mower cuts the grass in its season, Death, the grim leveler, sweeps away the human race at the appointed time. Behold, what havoc the Scythe of Time has made in the generations of man! If by chance we should escape the numerous evils incident to childhood and youth, and with health and vigor, to the years of manhood, yet, withal, we must soon be cut down by the all-devouring Scythe of Time, and be gathered into the land where our fathers have gone before us.

THE EMBLEMS OF MORTALITY.—At first view these emblems, the Setting-Maul, the Spade, the Coffin, the Open Grave, and the Sprig of Evergreen at its head, seem but to add shades of gloom to those that have just been moralized upon, the Hour-glass and the Scythe. Alas! who can look within an Open Grave without a sensation of profoundest melancholy? Is it for us, we mournfully ask, to resign our manhood and court the companionship of the worm? Must our eyes, trained to enjoy the charms of nature and of art, be blinded with these clods, our tongues silenced in this narrow receptacle? Yes, such will be our doom.

> A flowing river or a standing lake
> May their dry banks and naked shores forsake;
> Their waters may exhale and upward move,
> Their channel leave, to roll in clouds above:
> But the returning winter will restore
> What in the summer they had lost before;
> But if, O man, thy vital streams desert
> Their purple channels and defraud the heart,
> With fresh recruits they ne'er can be supplied,
> Nor feel their leaping life's returning tide.

And such are all the lessons of human life. We walk from grave to grave, as one may walk over a hard-fought battle-field, and find no place for his foot save upon the image of his kind. The emblems before us demand the tear of fraternal sympathy, and we can not refuse to weep. The frosts of death have palsied his mortal tenement. "There is hope of a tree if it be cut down that it may sprout again: but man dieth and wasteth away; yea, man giveth up the ghost, and where is he?"

As Freemasonry, in its three degrees, is an epitome of human life, so one who passes through its impressive ceremonial remains at the last under deep impressions of the certainty of death and the loathsomeness of the grave. But here steps in the qualified instructor of the Lodge, the Master, and the sad symbology opens out a brighter lesson. It opens out the brightest, clearest, most hopeful lesson of all; for it tells us what in the olden time was a Masonic secret; but now, "since light and immortality have been brought to light in the Gospel," is preached to every man, that, as this world is to the good man but the tiling-room of heaven, so the grave is the door of the Celestial Lodge where our GRAND MASTER and the multitude of the faithful who have entered before us are waiting to receive us with tokens of affection and songs of transport. The soul remains unaffected, flourishing in immortality.

Yea, though the body may decay into dust, and the dust be scattered to the four winds; though our name and our memory may fade from the minds of men, yet there is One pledged to remember us; to awaken us when the morning hour shall come; to reach forth His strong hand and to assist us to arise from our long sleep. The Lion of the Tribe of Judah hath prevailed! The Omnipotent is the All-merciful. We shall rise again.

> Tuba mirum spargens sonum,
> Per sepulchra regionum
> Coget omnes ante Thronum.

CHARITY.—The shining virtue of Charity, so honorable to our nature and so frequently enjoined in the Holy Volume upon our altars, will appropriately close this chapter. There are none of the characteristics of the ancient Craft so much valued as this; their earliest records and their perpetual practice coincide in this particular. Charity includes a supreme love to God and an ardent affection for the rational beings of his creation. This humane, generous, heaven-inspired principle is diametrically opposed to the prime ingredient of human nature, which looks only to self; not until this latter passion is supplanted by the former, will the soul of man be purified and fitted for the society of heaven. The feelings of the heart, guided by reason, should direct the hand of charity.

The true objects of relief are merit in distress, virtue in temptation, innocence in tears, industrious men borne down by affliction, acts of providence, widows left dependent and desolate, and orphans thrown in tender years upon the frigid charities of the world.

Thus we close our comments upon the symbolical degrees. Every step in this part of the Masonic Ladder will lift up the initiate further above the sordid level of humanity, and nearer to the celestial world, whose light, shining upon him through the first great light of the Order, wins him toward itself. Glorious system, which, while it the better fits a man for living in this world, so perfectly fits him for the world to come; and, dying late and honored, justifies us in pronouncing over his remains such a eulogy as this:

So falls the last of the old forest trees,
Within whose shades we wandered with delight;
Moss-grown, and hoary, yet the birds of heaven
Loved in its boughs to linger and to sing;
The summer winds made sweetest music there;
The soft, spring showers hung their brightest drops,
Glistening and cheerful on the mossy spray,
And to the last, that vigorous, ancient oak
Teemed with ripe fruitage!

Now the builders mourn
Through Temple-chambers their Grand Master fallen;
The clear intelligence, the genial soul,
The lips replete with wisdom, gone, all gone;
The ruffian Death has met and struck his prey,
And from the Quarry to the Mount all mourn.

Bind up with asphodel the mystic tools
And Jewels of the Work: bind up, ye Crafts,

The *Square;* it marked the fullness of his life;
To virtue's angle all his deeds were true;
The *Level*, lo! it leads us to the grave,
Thrice-honored, where our aged Father sleeps;
The *Plumb*, it points the home his soul has found;
He ever walked by this unerring line,
Let down, suggestive from the hand of God:
Bind up, in mourning dark and comfortless
The *Gauge*, he gave one part to God, and God,
In blest exchange, gave him eternity:
The *Trowel*, in his brotherly hand it spread
Sweet concord, joining long-estranged hearts;
The *Hour-glass*, whence his vital sands have fled,
And every grain denoting one good deed:
The *Gavel*, in his master-hand it swayed
For three-score years the moral architects,
Quelling all strife, directing every hand,
And pointing all to the great Builder, God!

Bind these with asphodel; enshroud these Tools
And Jewels of the Work; let bitterest tears
Flow for the man who wielded them so well,
But, overborne with Death, hath, in ripe age,
His labor fully done, passed from our sight!

CLOSING THOUGHTS ON THIS DEGREE.—A Lodge pursuing its work upon the design, and in the spirit of the foregoing lessons, will realize the virtue expressed by the poet in the following lines:

Where hearts are warm with kindred fire,
And love beams free from answering eyes,
Bright spirits hover always there
And that's the home the Masons prize.
The Mason's Home; ah, peaceful home!
The Home of love and light and joy;
How gladly does the Mason come
To share his tender, sweet employ.

All round the world, by land, by sea,
  Where summers burn or winters chill,
The exiled Mason turns to thee,
  And yearns to share the joys we feel.
    The Mason's Home; ah, happy home!
      The home of light and love and joy;
    There's not an hour but I would come
      And share this tender, sweet employ.

A weary task, a dreary round,
  Is all benighted man may know;
But here a brighter scene is found,
  The brightest scene that's found below.
    The Mason's Home; ah, blissful home!
      Glad center of unmingled joy;
    Long as I live, I'll gladly come
      And share this tender, sweet employ.

And when the hour of death shall come
  And darkness seal my closing eye,
May hands fraternal bear me home,
  The home where weary Masons lie.
    The Mason's Home; ah, heavenly home,
      To faithful hearts eternal joy:
    How blest to find beyond the tomb
      The end of all our sweet employ!

THE SECOND ORDER IN FREEMASONRY.

THE CAPITULAR DEGREES:

CONSISTING OF

THE MARK MASTER, THE PAST MASTER, THE MOST EXCELLENT MASTER, AND THE ROYAL ARCH MASON.

THESE four Degrees are conferred, according to the American system, in Lodges and a *Chapter of Capitular Masonry.* The ballot is taken in the Fourth or Royal Arch Degree, the same rules of balloting being observed as in the Symbolical Lodge. All discipline exercised by a Lodge requiring suspension and expulsion, is indorsed by the Chapter without inquiry. The Chapter has also its own code of discipline for offenses against its laws. Not less than nine members can open, work, or close a Royal Arch Chapter.

THE MARK MASTER.

THE MARK MASTER GLORIFIED.

God trusts to each a portion of his plan,
  And doth for honest labor wages give;
Wisdom and time he granteth every man,
  And will not idleness and sloth forgive.
The week is waning fast—art thou prepared,
O laborer, for the Overseer's award?

Hast thou been waiting in the market here,
  Because no man hath hired thee? Rise and go:
The sun on the Meridian doth appear—
  The Master calls thee to his service now;
Rise up, and go wherever duty calls,
And build with fervency the Temple-walls.

I see, within the heavenly home above,
  One who hath done his life-tasks faithfully;
In the dark quarries all the week he strove,
  And bore the heat and burden of the day;
So, when life's sun passed downward to the west,
Richest refreshment was his lot, and rest.

So shall it be with thee, O toiling one!
  However hard thine earthly lot may seem;
It is not long until the set of sun,
  And then the past will be a pleasing dream.
The Sabbath to the faithful laborer given,
Is blest companionship, and rest, and heaven.

THE MARK MASTER.

THE THEORY OF THE DEGREE OF MARK MASTER.

In entering upon a new system of Masonry, the *chapitral* or *capitular*, distinct in almost every particular from the *ancient* or *symbolical* system, a different style of elucidation must be adopted. We can not any longer look to *emblems* or *symbols* as our guides, because there are few characters of this sort applicable to these Degrees. Such *designs* as ingenious ritualists of the present day have introduced are inconvenient for reference, and will be thoroughly explained within these pages, but they can not, in a Masonic sense, be styled *symbols* or *emblems.* The distinction between Symbolical Masonry, or the Masonry of the Ancient Craft Degrees, and this, which forms the subject-matter of the present and subsequent pages, is, that the one is fixed and bounded by ancient *devices* called *symbols*, mostly of an architectural character, so definite in their character that it is impossible to innovate greatly upon them without detection; the other is controlled only by traditions, more or less apocryphal, which receive new forms, as the fancy of modern ritualists may treat them. Thus it follows that while the Ancient Craft Degrees are essentially uniform throughout the world, the Degrees conferred in the Chapters and Councils in the United States are essentially different from those which, under similar names, are worked in foreign countries.

But with all this confusion of working, liability to innovation, and want of antiquity, there is something so beautiful in the *drama* of the following Degrees, the *covenants* are so impressive and humane, and the *lessons* inculcated in the various Lectures so fragrant with the spirit of the Divine Word, that it need not be wondered at if, in the United States at least, where the reverence for antiquity is less than in older countries, they are prized equally with the ancient and world-wide system. Almost every Master Mason in this country is, or intends to become, a Royal Arch Mason, and a Mason of the Cryptic Rite.

What we have said in general terms of the six following Degrees, (the Mark Master, the Past Master, the Most Excellent Master, the Royal Arch Mason, the Royal Master, and the Select Master,) we affirm with peculiar emphasis of the Degree of MARK MASTER. Its *drama* is exquisitely beautiful, exhibiting the work of the scholar, the Christian, the Biblical student, and the genius, who, had he turned his mind to dramatic writings, might even have emulated a Shakspeare. Its *covenants* are benevolent in an eminent degree, being admirably designed for the furtherance of that social and charitable intercourse between brethren which this Degree particularly enjoins. Its *lessons*, as the following pages will show, are wisely culled from the great treasury of the Divine Word. In brief, so practical is the MARK MASTER'S DEGREE in its character, as conferred in the United States, that its principal device, THE KEY-STONE, is publicly worn, bearing the same relation to the so-called "Higher Degrees" which the symbol of the SQUARE AND COMPASS bears to the "Lower Degrees."

In theory, the Degree of MARK MASTER is appendant to that of Fellow Craft, and, could its traditions be historically established, might, with propriety, be conferred upon Fellow Crafts as the complement of that grade. Its *original members* were merely Fellow Crafts; its *lectures* describe the manner in which Fellow Crafts were classified, governed, and paid; its *covenants* have direct application to Fellow Crafts alone. But, by general consent, the Degree in this country is confined to Master Masons alone, and a new system of Lodges is framed to accommodate it. The title of the organization in which the Degrees of Mark Master, Past Master, Most Excellent Master, and Royal Arch Mason are conferred, is *Royal Arch Chapter.* In a Chapter, not less than nine members can open or work. The government of Chapters is intrusted to *Grand Chapters of Capitular or Chapitral Masonry,* of which there is one in every State in the Union.

MARK MASTER'S LODGE AND JEWELS.

THE ALTAR.—The central design in this, as in all preceding Lodges, is the Altar, surmounted with God's revealed Law, crowned with the Masonic implements—the Square and Compass. To an observing eye, this constant recurrence of sacred emblems must be highly suggestive. Can an institution be evil in tendency that seeks the blessing of God through every grade of its advancement? Can the secrecy of which the enemies of

Freemasonry make a handle, be of an improper character when, whatever else is shut out of the hall, *God is not shut out?*

There is a prayer unsaid—
No lips its accents move;
'Tis uttered by the pleading eye,
And registered above.

Each mystic Sign is prayer,
By hand of Mason given;
Each gesture pleads or imprecates,
And is observed in heaven.

The deeds that mercy prompts
Are *prayers* in sweet disguise;
Though unobserved by any here,
They're witnessed in the skies.

Then at the Altar kneel—
In silence make thy prayer;
And He whose very name is love,
The plea will surely hear.

The darkest road is light—
We shun the dangerous snare,
When heavenly hand conducts the way,
Responsive to our prayer.

THE KEY-STONE.—The use of the *key-stone* as a symbolical device is peculiar to the MARK MASTER. Originally connected with a pleasing tradition, upon which the Degree is principally founded, it has become the distinctive emblem of the grade; and the members are impressively instructed to mark well its figurative explanation. Upon its front are engraven, within two concentric circles, certain cryptographic characters, known only to the initiated, but bearing a general allusion to that "hieroglyphic bright" on the Fellow Crafts' tracing board, which, in the language of the poet-brother, Burns,

> "None but craftsmen ever saw."

Within the inmost circle is a space left for the private "Mark" of the member who displays the badge. This is some device selected by himself, having reference to his avocation in life, his heraldic bearings, or such figure as is dictated by his fancy. According to the general rule of Mark Masters' Lodges, every member is required to choose a "Mark" within a specified time after entrance upon the grade. Such "Mark" must not conflict with one previously chosen by a member of the same Lodge; and, being once recorded in the "Mark Book," can not afterward be changed, save by consent of the Lodge.

The use of this "Mark" in those dispensations of benevolence which form so striking a feature in this system of Masonry, is exceedingly significant. Its perversion is carefully guarded against: no MARK MASTER may pledge his "Mark" the second time until it has been redeemed from its former pledge; and the plea of distress made by a MARK MASTER, when accompanied by his "Mark," can not be refused by a member of this grade without violating the covenant of the Degree.

> Fairest and foremost of the train that wait
> On man's most dignified and happy state,
> Whether we name thee *Charity* or *Love*,
> Chief grace below, and all in all above—
> O, never seen but in thy blest effects,
> Or felt but in the soul that Heaven selects;
> Who seeks to praise thee, and to make thee known
> To other hearts, must have thee in his own.

Teach me to feel another's woe—
To hide the faults I see;
That mercy I to others show,
That mercy show to me.

No works shall find acceptance in that day
When all disguises shall be rent away,
That square not truly with the Scripture plan,
Nor spring from love to God or love to man.

THE THREE SQUARES.—In the Degree of Fellow Craft, of which this of the MARK MASTER is but the complement, the Masonic application of the Square is explained. As applied to the person of a candidate for Masonic light, the Square expresses that he must be physically, mentally, and morally perfect, to be able to pass the strict ordeal of Ancient Craft Masonry. The three squares used in the Lodge of MARK MASTERS have the same general reference, but in a more extended and threefold sense. Here the *works* of each member are considered as applied to the squares of the Divine Law in the three dispensations: the Patriarchal, the Mosaic, and the Christian. The grand trial of humanity to be had at the last day, when God

"Shall try the blocks we offer with his own unerring square,"

is forcibly expressed, and an inimitable moral drawn. There is impressed upon every member the duty of being circumspect in all his words and actions, and of discountenancing immorality in others, as well as of keeping his own white apron untarnished by a single stain. It was written by the pen of inspiration, under the dictation of the unerring wisdom of the Most High, that *virtue exalteth a nation;* and it is equally true that vice or immorality, unrestrained, is not only a reproach on any institution where it is allowed to exist, but will, sooner or later, destroy the peace and happiness of the members of that institution. MARK MASTERS, therefore, are taught so to conduct themselves, in their intercourse with each other as brethren, as well as in their dealings with the world without, that they may not bring discredit upon themselves or the institution of Masonry to which they belong.

THE HAPPY HOUR.

O, happy hour when Masons meet!
O, rarest joys when Masons greet!
Each interwoven with the other,
And brother truly joined with brother
In intercourse that none can daunt—
Linked by the ties of covenant.

See, ranged about the Holy Word,
The Craftsmen praise their common Lord!
See in each eye a love well proven,
Around each heart a faith well woven!
Feel in each hand-grip what a tie
Is this that men call Masonry!

Blest bond! when broken, we would fain
Unite the severed links again;
Would urge the tardy hours along,
To spend the wealth of light and song,
That makes the Lodge a sacred spot.
O, be the season ne'er forgot,
That takes us from the world of care
To happy halls where Masons are!

THE CEDARS OF LEBANON.

Palestine, as a territory, is destitute of forests suitable for building material. When, therefore, King David projected a grand edifice which should be the crowning glory of the reign of his son Solomon, and an evidence of the national devotion to God, he made application to Hiram, the Phœnician monarch, whose possessions included the powerful mountain ranges of Lebanon, for a supply of the cedars which grew there in unparalleled abundance. The Tyrian king, between whom and King David there existed a more than royal friendship, readily acceded to his request; and thus the work of preparation for building was expedited. So large was the supply of this material furnished to King Solomon, that, after the completion of the edifice upon Mount Moriah, which occupied seven years and upward, King Solomon erected, upon the contiguous hill westward, a palace for his own use, in which, so abundantly did the cedar enter, that it was entitled "the House of Lebanon."

On Lebanon's majestic brow
The grand and lofty cedars grew
That, shipped in floats to Joppa's port,
Up to Jerusalem were brought.

The principal groves of cedar were found about one hundred and fifty miles north-west of Jerusalem, and not far from the sea-coast on which the cities of Sidon, Sarepta, and Tyre stood. This suggests the mode of transhipment, which is described in the Scriptures: The trunks of trees were rudely shaped, made into floats or rafts, and brought down the coast by Phœnician mariners, the most skillful sailors of the age, about one hundred miles to the port of Joppa, the only seaport opposite Jerusalem, from which it was distant but thirty-five miles. Here they were adapted, by the tools of the workmen, to the exact places they were to occupy in the Temple, and then carried by land to the Sacred Hill.

Being incorruptible to atmospheric influences, the cedar beams and planks thus used might have remained to this day, the ornaments of Moriah and Sion, and the tokens of the brotherly covenants that connected the monarchs of Israel and Phœnicia, but for the destructive influences of invasion. The Temple, having stood four hundred and sixteen years, was burned by Nebuchadnezzar, King of Babylon, who was the instrument in God's hand to chastise a rebellious and idolatrous people.

The number of cedars remaining upon Lebanon is very small—less, it is said, than one hundred; but these are grand specimens of the Creator's power, towering in sublimity in the valleys, where they are hidden, and suggesting what must have been the ancient glory of Lebanon, covered with a growth of such.

JOPPA.—The peculiarly hilly, and even precipitous, character of Joppa is preserved in the traditions of the Degree of MARK MASTER, and a benevolent moral deduced, in accordance with the entire instructions of the grade.

True charity, a plant divinely nursed,
Fed by the hope from which it rose at first,
Thrives against hope, and in the rudest scene;
Storms but enliven its unfading green;
Exuberant is the shadow it supplies;
Its fruit on earth, its growth above the skies.

Thus no opportunity is lost, either in covenants, emblems, traditions, or dramatic exercises, to impress upon the candidate's mind the Divine lesson that, great as faith and hope are esteemed in their effects upon the human heart, "the greatest of these is charity."

The White Stone.—Many references are made in this Degree to "the white stone," "the head-stone," "the stone which the builders rejected," "the head of the corner." The whole of this, however, is most impressively conveyed in the following passage from Revelations: "To him that overcometh will I give to eat of the hidden manna, and will give him a white stone, and in the stone a new name written, which no man knoweth saving him that receiveth it."

The Method of Vigilance.—The vast numbers of workmen who labored upon the Temple—more than one hundred and fifty thousand—will suggest to the mind some of the difficulties encountered in rewarding merit by a fair compensation to the laborers, and punishing the guilty, both those who idly dissipated their time, and those who attempted, through fraud, to secure wages which they had not earned. These difficulties, quite insuperable to an ordinary mind, were thoroughly obviated by the wisdom of Solomon, and it is believed that no instance of impropriety occurred, during the whole labor, which was not summarily detected and punished. From the traditions in which these matters are communicated, speculative Masons derive moral instruction, apt, abounding, and important.

The Working Tools.—The implements of practical architecture, adopted as appropriate to this Degree, are the chisel and the mallet. The former suggests the effects of discipline and education upon the human heart, in discovering the latent virtues of the mind, drawing them forth to range the large field of matter and space, and displaying the summit of human knowledge, viz., our duty to God and to man.

The latter suggests that, in the school of discipline, a man may learn to be content. What the mallet is to the workman, enlightened reason is to the passions; it curbs ambition, it depresses envy, it moderates anger, and it encourages good dispositions.

THE DIVINE LAW OF JUSTICE.—In the ceremony of closing the Lodge of MARK MASTERS is introduced the parable of the householder, who employed laborers, as he found them in waiting in the market-place, to do the work of his vineyard. To each he proffers a specified rate of wages upon which the labor was performed. And when, at the close of day, he called together the workmen, and, paying them the covenanted compensation, he found some dissatisfied with the distribution, not because there had been any breach of the contract, but because the laborers of but an hour were receiving as much as those who had borne the burden and heat of the day, the householder silenced their unreasonable complaints by reference to the Divine law of justice.

THE CLOSING INJUNCTIONS.—To the candidate who has passed thoughtfully through the dramatic ceremonial of the MARK MASTER'S DEGREE, fortunate in having a well-instructed Master and an expert membership, the closing injunctions appeal with great power. In the honorable character of MARK MASTER, it is more particularly your duty to endeavor to let your conduct in the Lodge and among the brethren be such as may stand the test of the

Grand Overseer's Square, that you may not, like the unfinished and imperfect work of the negligent and unfaithful of former times, be rejected and thrown aside as unfit for that spiritual building, that house not made with hands, eternal in the heavens.

While such is your conduct, should misfortune assail you, should friends forsake you, should envy traduce your good name, and malice persecute you, yet may you have confidence, that among MARK MASTERS you will find friends who will administer relief to your distresses and comfort your afflictions; ever bearing in mind, as a consolation under all the frowns of fortune and as an encouragement to hope for better prospects, that the stone which the builders rejected, possessing merits to them unknown, became the chief stone of the corner.

THE PAST MASTER.

THE PAST MASTER.

O! raised to oriental chair,
With royal honors crowned,
The grace and dignity to bear,
As in the days renowned.
Let firmness guide the ruling hand,
Nor Gavel fall in vain;
And kindness soften the command,
And law the vice restrain.

The open Word delight to read—
That trestle-board of heaven—
And see that every Mason heed
The deathless precepts given;
And let the Trowel truly spread
Its cement so divine,
That all the Craft be duly paid
Their corn, and oil, and wine.

The Plumb-line, hanging from the sky,
In the GRAND MASTER's hand,
Be this your emblem, ever nigh,
By this to walk and stand;
Thus grateful Craftsmen will conspire
To sing your praises true,
And honors grant you, even higher,
Than now they offer you.

THE PAST MASTER.

THE THEORY OF THE DEGREE OF PAST MASTER.

WHAT we have said of the dramatic beauty of the various degrees elucidated in these pages, does not apply to this of PAST MASTER so much as to the others. Its drama is but slight, but a single lesson being communicated therein, viz., that of the proper government of Lodges by Masters. What it lacks in dramatic force, however, is supplied in the importance of the subject. Nothing is more vital to the prosperity of Freemasonry than the proper instruction of Lodge-masters.

All Masonic history is uniform in the expression of this fact. Mr. Webb, in his remarks upon the Degree of PAST MASTER, says:

"It should be carefully studied and well understood by every Master of a Lodge. It treats of the government of our society and the disposition of our rulers, and illustrates their requisite qualifications. It includes the ceremony of opening and closing Lodges in the several preceding Degrees, and also the forms of installation and consecration in the Grand Lodge, as well as private Lodges. It comprehends the ceremonies at laying the foundation-stones of public buildings, and also at dedications and at funerals, by a variety of particulars explanatory of those ceremonies."

The form of government adopted in Masonry is peculiar to itself. While the members of a Lodge are unrestricted in their prerogative of electing, annually, their Master, such an one as they prefer, yet, from the moment of his installation, they resign the management of their Masonic affairs unreservedly into his hands. He is the custodian of their landmarks. From his authority there is no appeal, save to the Grand Master. There can be no meeting of the Lodge without his approbation, as the visible emblem of authority; *the Charter or Warrant,* without which the Lodge can not legally assemble, is in his possession. The Lodge has no representatives in Grand Lodge save himself and the two Wardens, nor can these be ousted from the privilege of representation by any action of the Lodge. This sketch of the Master's relation to the brethren will show that his station is widely different from that of the chairman or president of an ordinary association.

Such being the ancient powers and prerogatives of the Master, it is important that they should be carefully hedged around and determined beyond cavil; also that he should be thoroughly instructed in them. That a spirit of dictation and haughtiness is likely to grow out of so large a range of authority, is highly probable; and some means of communication between the Lodge-master and others who hold, or have heretofore held, similar authority, must be admitted as very desirable. It is for these purposes the Degree of PAST MASTER is designed.

DISPENSING WAGES.—One of the prime duties of a Master is that of "paying the Craft their wages," conveyed in the following verses:

They come from many a pleasant home,
To do the ancient work they come,
  With cheerful hearts, and light;
They leave the outer world a space,
And, gathering here in secret place,
  They spend the social night
They earn the meed of honest toil,
Wages of corn, and wine, and oil.

Upon the sacred altar lies
Ah! many a sacrifice,
  Made by these working men:
The passions curbed, the lusts restrained,
And hands with human gore unstained,
  And hearts from envy clean;
They earn the meed of honest toil,
Wages of corn, and wine, and oil.

They do the deeds their MASTER did;
The naked clothe, the hungry feed—
  They warm the shivering poor;
They wipe from fevered eyes the tear;
A brother's joys and griefs they share,
  As ONE had done before;
They earn the meed of honest toil,
Wages of corn, and wine, and oil.

Show them how Masons Masons know,
The land of strangers journeying through;
  Show them how Masons love;
And let admiring spirits see
How reaches Mason's charity
  From earth to heaven above;
Give them the meed of honest toil,
Wages of corn, and wine, and oil.

Then will each brother's tongue declare
How bounteous his wages are;
  And peace will reign within;
Your walls with skillful hands will grow,
And coming generations know
  Your Temple is Divine;
Then give the meed of honest toil,
Wages of corn, and wine, and oil.

Yes, pay these men their just desert;
Let none dissatisfied depart,
  But give them full reward;
Give light, that longing eyes may see;
Give truth, that doth from error free;
  Give them to know the Lord!
This is their meed of honest toil,
Wages of corn, and wine, and oil.

The Burial of the Dead.—Another of the primary duties of the Lodge-master is that of a decorous burial of the fraternal dead. This is a subject of so much importance as to demand the best efforts of those to whom it is intrusted. All the symbolisms of Freemasonry point to the grave and the shining world beyond for their explication. This is the most impressive ceremony of the Order that can be performed in public. It has in it all the elements of dramatic effect—the dead body, the sorrowing mourners, the coffin, the spade, the sprig of evergreen, the open grave. The ritualists, Preston and Webb, whose plans are mainly followed in the United States, give a burial service sufficiently impressive. It only remains for the Lodge-master to lay the subject impressively before the eyes and ears of his congregation. It has been well said that "a Masonic burial, properly performed, is productive of twelve Masonic initiations," so deep is the impression made on the minds of the community.

MASONIC CONSECRATIONS.—At the consecration of foundation-stones, cape-stones, etc., done under Masonic auspices, the Lodge-master likewise takes the lead, either as the representative of his own Lodge or of the Grand Lodge.

THE DISCIPLINE OF THE LODGE.—The discipline of the Lodge being essentially in the Lodge-master's care, he is strictly charged, in his own installation service, in fifteen ancient regulations, hedging him so closely about that he can not materially err. These are, in brief, that he shall be a good and moral man; that he will be peaceable and law-abiding; that he will avoid plots and conspiracies; that he will respect the civil magistrate, work diligently, live creditably, and act honorably by all men; that he will honor the Masonic rulers, and submit to their awards; that he will avoid private quarrels, and cherish temperance; that he will be cautious, courteous, and faithful; that he will respect the true brethren and discountenance the false; that he will promote the general good of society, cultivate the social virtues, and propagate the knowledge of Masonry; that he will pay homage to the Grand Master, and conform to the lawful edicts of the Grand Lodge; that he will suffer no innovations in the body of Masonry; that he will attend the sessions of Grand Lodge; that he will permit no new Lodge to be formed save by consent of Grand Lodge, and give no countenance to clandestine Masonry; that he will admit no man a Mason without cautious scrutiny into character; and that he will put visitors to due examination before admission.

THE TEMPLE OF SOLOMON.

The PAST MASTER has his own traditions relative to King Solomon and his Temple. The following is the scriptural account of this edifice:

"The house which King Solomon built for the Lord, the length thereof was threescore cubits, and the breadth thereof twenty cubits, and the height thereof thirty cubits. And the porch before the temple of the house, twenty cubits was the length thereof, according to the breadth of the house; and ten cubits was the breadth thereof before the house. And for the house he made windows of narrow lights. And against the wall of the house he built chambers round about, against the walls of the house round about, both of the temple and of the oracle: and he made chambers round about. The nethermost chamber was five cubits broad, and the middle was six cubits broad, and the third was seven cubits broad: for without, in the wall of the house, he made narrowed rests round about, that the beams should not be fastened in the walls of the house. And in the eleventh year, in the month Bul, (which is the eighth month,) was the house finished throughout all the parts thereof, and according to all the fashion of it. So was he seven years in building it."—1 Kings vi.

The above account, though doubtless in accordance with the architectural nomenclature of the period, is almost inexplicable at the present day. Various plans have been drawn by skillful artists, designed to afford to the eye a view of the shape and proportions of this remarkable edifice, but there is so little harmony among the plans as to lead to the suspicion that the key to the architectural designs of Solomon has not yet been discovered. The ground on which it stood is a part of Mount Moriah, near the place where the faith of Abraham was tried when he was commanded to offer his son Isaac upon the altar, and where David appeased the destroying angel by erecting an altar in the threshing-floor of Araunah. It was begun in the year of the world 2992, and before the Christian era 1012; and, as the Biblical narrative positively asserts, was completed in about seven years. In its construction, Solomon engaged the coöperation of Hiram, the King of Tyre, and of the most skillful artist of that, and, perhaps, of any age, called, it is said, in the Phœnician dialect, Abdonemus, but, in the ancient Masonic constitutions, Amom, or Hiram Abiff, as his Assistant Grand Master of the work. Under them were 200 Hadorim, or princes; 3,300 Menatzchim, or expert Master Masons, as overseers; 80,000 Ghiblim (sculptors), Ishchotzeb, (hewers), and Benai (layers), who were ingenious Fellow Crafts, besides a levy out of all Israel of 30,000, under Adoniram, the Junior Grand Warden, making in all 113,600, exclusive of the two Grand Wardens employed in the noble undertaking. Besides these, there were 70,000 Ishsabal, or men of burden.

Collection of Masonic Implements.—The general collection of Masonic implements, placed before the eye of the Worshipful Master, reminds him of his power and jurisdiction, while it warns him to avoid the abuse of that power, limiting his jurisdiction and prescribing his conduct. These emblems afford him copious topics of advice to such as assist him in the government of the Fraternity, as well as to all the brethren over whom he is called to preside. There he can descant upon the excellencies of the Holy Writings as the rule of life; for those writings teach us, that, being born upon a Level, we should act upon the Square, circumscribing our desires within the Compass of nature's gifts, poured upon us from the Horn of Plenty. Here, also, he may exhort them to walk uprightly, suffering neither the pressure of poverty nor the avarice of riches to tempt the heart to swerve for a moment from the Line of rectitude suspended before them from the center of heaven. The division of time into equal and regular portions, and the subjection of our passions and desires, will come naturally up, while the by-laws of the Lodge regulate the deportment of the Craft assembled for purposes of social improvement and mental recreation. Thus the Master will demand prompt obedience, while he exercises an affectionate moderation. He will mingle the sweetness of mercy with the necessary severity of justice.

THE MOST EXCELLENT MASTER.

HUMBLE ADORATION.

PROSTRATE before the Lord,
 We praise and bless his name,
That he doth condescend to own
 The temple that we frame.

No winter's piercing blast,
 No summer's scorching flame
Has daunted us; and prostrate here,
 We praise and bless his name.

From lofty Lebanon
 These sacred cedars came;
We dedicate them to thy cause,
 And praise and bless thy name.

Each noble block complete,
 Each pure and sparkling gem,
We give to build and beautify,
 And praise and bless thy name.

With millions here below,
 With heaven's own cherubim,
Prostrate before the fire and cloud,
 We praise and bless thy name.

THE MOST EXCELLENT MASTER.

THE THEORY OF THE DEGREE OF MOST EXCELLENT MASTER.

THE glowing eulogiums pronounced in a preceding page upon the Degree of Mark Master are equally appropriate when applied to that of MOST EXCELLENT MASTER. Its *drama*, *covenants*, and *lectures* bear marks of the same skillful hand that framed the other, while the Scriptural fact conveyed in them—that of the completion and dedication of King Solomon's Temple—is even more impressive in its character.

The Degree of MOST EXCELLENT MASTER has always been a favorite in the United States since the period of its introduction, some seventy years ago.

When the work of the building was complete, the timbers brought from the distant forests, the stones from the nearer quarries, the jewels from Ethiopian mines, the precious metals from every part of the known earth—when, amidst an assembled multitude enumerated by millions, the Wise King stood up to dedicate a work in which skill and wealth had been exhausted, incidents occurred of a Divine character which gave token of God's acceptance of the offering. The FIRE and the CLOUD from heaven descended—the one to veil from human eyes the master-piece of human glory, the other to consume the multitude of burnt-offerings which the piety of the chosen people had accumulated upon the altar. Then the multitude of Israel fell prostrate in profoundest adoration. Then from every voice there went up the grand *So mote it be* of the Masonic heart, "For he is good; for his mercy endureth forever!"

These things are taught in the drama of the MOST EXCELLENT MASTER'S DEGREE. The spirit of the *Dedication Prayer* is the spirit of this grade, wherein King Solomon stood before the altar of the Lord, in the presence of all the congregation of Israel, and spread forth his hands toward heaven, and blessed the Lord God of Israel in fitting terms as a covenant-keeping God. Then, in a series of seven petitions, he asked:

1. That the Temple might become a holy place, in which perjury should ever be detected and punished.

2. That Israel, stricken at any time before the enemy for their sins, if they should turn toward the Temple and confess, pray, and make supplication to God, might be forgiven and brought again to the land of their fathers.

3. That the rains of heaven, restrained on account of Israel's offenses, should be restored to the land whenever the people thereof should turn to the Temple, confess, pray, and make supplication.

4. That famine, pestilence, blasting, mildew, locust, and caterpillar, blasting and devastating the land of Israel, should be removed whenever the people thereof should turn to the Temple, confess, pray, and make supplication.

5. That the stranger, coming from a far country for His Name's sake, and praying toward the Temple, should

be heard in heaven, and the purpose of his supplications fully granted.

6. That Israel, going forth to battle, first turning to the Temple and praying to him who dwelleth therein, might be heard in heaven and their prayer granted.

7. That Israel, being carried away out of the country, captives, to a country near or far, on account of their sins, but returning to God in heart and soul, and praying to God toward the land of their fathers, and the city of God's choice, and the Temple built for His Name, might receive compassion from their conquerors, be forgiven for their offenses, and all their prayers answered and granted.

These seven grand requests being proffered in the hearing of the assembled millions, King Solomon now solemnly blessed all the congregation of Israel with a loud voice, saying:

"The Lord our God be with us as he was with our fathers.

"Let him not leave us nor forsake us.

"Let these words of supplication be nigh unto the Lord day and night, that he may maintain the cause of his servant and of his people Israel, at all times, as the matter shall require; that all the people of the earth may know that the Lord is God, and that there is none else.

"Let your heart, therefore, be perfect with the Lord our God, to walk in his statutes and to keep his commandments, as at this day."

THE PARTING COUNSEL.—The parting counsel given by the Royal Builder to those who for more than seven years had patiently served him, is suggested in the following lines:

King Solomon sat in his mystic chair—
His chair on a platform high—
And his words addressed,
Through the listening West,
To a band of brothers nigh—
Through the West and South
These words of truth,
To a band of brothers nigh.

Ye builders, go! ye have done the work—
The cape-stone standeth sure;
From the lowermost rock
To the loftiest block,
The fabric is secure—
From the arch's swell
To the pinnacle,
The fabric is secure.

Go, crowned with fame: old time will pass,
And many changes bring;
But the deed you've done,
The circling sun
Through every land will sing;
The moon and stars,
While earth endures,
Through every land will sing.

Go, build like this: from the quarries vast
The precious stones reveal;
There's many a block
In the matrice-rock,
Will honor your fabrics well;
There's many a beam
By the mountain stream,
Will honor your fabrics well.

Go, build like this: divest with skill
Each superfluity;

With critic eye
Each fault espy—
Be zealous, fervent, free;
By the perfect Square
Your work prepare—
Be zealous, fervent, free.

Go, build like this: to a fitting place
Raise up the Ashlars true;
On the trestle-board
Of your Master's Lord,
The grand intention view;
In each mystic line
Of the vast design,
The grand intention view.

Go, build like this: and when exact
The joinings scarce appear,
With the trowel's aid
Such cement spread,
As time can never wear;
Lay thickly round
Such wise compound
As time can never wear.

Go, brothers; thus enjoined, farewell;
Spread o'er the darkened West
Illume each clime
With art sublime—
The noblest truths attest;
Be Masters now;
And, as you go,
The noblest truths attest!

So Mote it Be.—This expression is the emphatic *amen* uttered by the assembled craft upon the repetition of any of the ancient landmarks. It is the positive affirmation of all that has been handed down to the existing generation by the fathers. The following lines express the spirit and intention of the words:

So mote it be with us when life shall end,
And from the East the Lord of Light shall bend;
And we, our six days' labor fully done,
Shall claim our wages at the MASTER's throne.

So mote it be with us: that when the Square,
That perfect implement, with heavenly care
Shall be applied to every block we bring,
No fault shall see our MASTER and our King.

So mote it be with us: that, though our days
Have yielded little to the Master's praise,
The little we have builded may be proved
To have the marks our first Grand MASTER loved!

So mote it be with us: we are but weak;
Our days are few; our trials who can speak!
But sweet is our communion while we live,
And rich rewards the MASTER deigns to give.

Let's toil, then, cheerfully; let's die in hope;
The wall in wondrous grandeur riseth up;
They who come after shall the work complete,
And they and we receive the wages meet.

THE KEY-STONE.—In the beautiful and affecting drama of the Mark Master's grade, reference is had to the key-stone, the name of its designer, its singular history and destination. In the grade of MOST EXCELLENT MASTER this charming device again comes to light, illustrating the completion of the edifice of Solomon. Considered as an arch, the placing of the key-stone represents its perfection. In the deeds of charity to which the principles of our ancient institution daily and hourly prompt us, who would like to feel that the last act of kindness he has performed should never be succeeded by another? that no further opportunity will ever be afforded him by the Master of life to wipe away a sorrowing tear, to soften an agonizing sigh, to mitigate a weight of woe? Yet, as human life is in the highest degree uncertain, such may be the case with any one of us. Already the fiat may have gone forth that the arch of our life is finished, and the vacant seat in the world to come waits our entrance to be filled! Already the sprig of Acacia, hanging greenly upon its native tree, may be marked out and designated, which the Master of our Lodge shall throw upon our coffin! Solemn reflection! let us improve it by improving every moment of our time to do good, so that when the key-stone is finally dropped into place, marking the consummation of earthly things, we may expect, both from our GRAND MASTER above, and from his surrounding angels and spirits, a welcome into the seats of the blest.

THE LIGHT OF THE TEMPLE.—To one whose shadow fills the earth, whose purpose was no less than that of fixing Jehovah, the light and life of heaven, in a tenement of earth; whose site, so wisely chosen, refreshes our memory with the faith of a patriarch, the repentance of a king, the sacrifice of a Redeemer; whose preparation exhausted the treasures of the wealthiest and the zeal of the mightiest; whose pattern, conceived in the Divine mind, was traced by the finger and communicated in writing by the spirit of God—that spirit which can not err; whose builders, divinely selected, divinely inspired, were divinely strengthened and sustained; whose completion left nothing wanting, introduced nothing superfluous; whose dedication called down from heaven the fire of approval and the cloud of acceptance; whose memory is both the pride and the sting of the Hebrew as he walks his homeless, aimless way upon the earth: to such a theme—to one that directs us to the fountain of life for sustenance and enjoyment; to one rich enough to comprehend Revelation, tradition, reference, type, antitype, prophecy and fulfillment; to one that challenges us to consider a Temple the most costly, the most beautiful, the most perfect, the most sacred, the most venerable ever contemplated, executed, or beautified by man—this Degree of MOST EXCELLENT MASTER directs our minds. It is good for the young laying up a store of useful knowledge, to be taught concerning Messiah's temple and Jehovah's altar. It is good for the Christian searching out the ways of God with man; for the worldling seeking the sublime and the beautiful; for the philosopher craving all knowledge that is high and ennobling—to be enlightened upon a topic like this.

THE ROYAL ARCH MASON.

O, WEARY hearts, so worn and desolate!
Torn from their native land, from ruined homes,
From desecrated shrines. O, hapless fate!
Better the solitude of Judah's tombs
Than all that Judah's foemen can bestow.
In the far land, where tuneless waters flow,
Along the sad Euphrates, as they sigh,
"Jerusalem!" "Jerusalem!" they cry,
"When we forget thee, city of our love,
May He forget, whose city is above;
And when we fail to speak thy matchless fame,
May He consign us to enduring shame!"

O, joyful spirits, now so bright and free,
Amidst the hallowed palm-trees of the west!
No more the exiles' want and misery,
The tuneless waters and the homes unblest;
Remember Sion now, her ruined shrine,
And take each manly form, the work divine;
Plant the foundation-stone; erect the spire
That shall send back in light the eastern fire;
Set up the altar, let the victim bleed,
To expiate each impious word and deed;
And tell the nations, when to Sion come,
"The Lord is God; He brought His people home!"

THE ROYAL ARCH MASON.

THE THEORY OF THE DEGREE OF ROYAL ARCH MASON.

WHATEVER degree of popularity the preceding Degrees of Mark Master and Most Excellent Master may have acquired, on account of their beauty of *drama*, their humane *covenants*, and the wisdom with which their *lectures* are framed, they must surrender the palm in all these respects to the one now before us, that of ROYAL ARCH MASON. Mr. Webb, who was mainly instrumental in introducing it, in its present form, into this country, says, in terms almost extravagant:

"It is indescribably more august, sublime, and important than all which precede it. It is the summit and perfection of ancient Masonry. It impresses on our mind a belief of the being and existence of a Supreme Deity, without beginning of days or end of years, and reminds us of the reverence due to His holy name."

To understand properly the theory of this elaborate and beautiful Degree, we must recall to mind the historical fact, more minutely described further on, that the temple of King Solomon, whose construction forms the subject-matter of the several Degrees of Entered Apprentice, Fellow Craft, Master Mason, Mark Master, and Most Excellent Master, was totally destroyed and leveled to its foundation by the Chaldeans, under Nebuchadnezzar, four hundred and nine years after its completion and dedication. The Jewish nation was carried into captivity to Babylon, where they remained for fifty-two years. Then a portion of them, led by Zerubbabel, returned to Jerusalem, by permission of the reigning king, and rebuilt the temple. This rebuilding, including the national history from the destruction of the first temple, nineteen years before, constitutes the basis of the ROYAL ARCH DEGREE. It can readily be seen, that in this broad field the ritualist had stirring matter to his hand; the destruction of the temple and city; the lamentable journey of eight hundred miles into captivity; the mournful exile, which even the singing of "the songs of Sion" could not enliven; the joyful return westward, when the days of captivity were ended; and the devoted, self-sacrificing labors of the reconstruction—all these, with subsidiary themes, which the genius of the ritualist could so readily intersperse, make up the grandest display of which the science of Freemasonry, ancient or modern, admits.

THE BANNERS OF THE TRIBES.

The grand march of the Israelites through the wilderness from Egypt to Canaan was conducted with an order and system truly admirable. Each tribe had a banner, with distinctive devices borrowed from the imagery employed in the death-bed prophecy of Jacob, (Gen. xlix.)

As these banners are of practical application in the instructions of the ROYAL ARCH MASON, we give them here in some detail.

1. REUBEN.—Jacob said of Reuben, "Thou art my first-born, my might, and the beginning of my strength, the excellency of dignity, and the excellency of power." The emblem inscribed on the banner of Reuben was that of *a young man in the prime of his strength.* The place of Reuben in the desert-encampment was on the south side. Simeon and Gad were his supporters. In the division of Canaan, the tribe of Reuben was stationed in the south-east, directly east of the Dead Sea.

2. SIMEON.—Jacob said of Simeon, "Instruments of cruelty are in his habitation. Cursed be his anger, for it was fierce; and his wrath, for it was cruel." The emblem inscribed on the banner of Simeon was *an instrument of war.* The place of Simeon in the desert-encampment was as a supporter of Reuben, on the south side. In the division of Canaan, the tribe of Simeon was stationed in the south-west, on the Mediterranean coast.

3. LEVI.—Jacob coupled Levi with Simeon in his stern rebuke, quoted above. The emblem inscribed on the banner of Levi was like that of Simeon, *an instrument of war.* This tribe, being made the sacerdotal tribe, its place in the desert-encampment was in the center, with the tabernacle of the congregation. In the division of Canaan, forty-eight towns and cities, with their suburbs, were allotted to Levi.

4. JUDAH.—Jacob said of Judah, "Thou art he whom thy brethren shall praise; thy hand shall be in the neck of thine enemies: thy father's children shall bow down before thee. Judah is a lion's whelp. He couched as

a lion, and as an old lion." The emblem incribed on the banner of Judah was *a couching lion under a crown and scepter.* The place of Judah in the desert-encampment was on the east side. Issachar and Zebulun were his supporters. In the division of Canaan, the tribe of Judah was stationed in the south.

5. Zebulun.—Jacob said of Zebulun, "He shall dwell at the haven of the sea, and he shall be for a haven of ships." The emblem inscribed on the banner of Zebulun was *a ship.* The place of Zebulun in the desert-encampment was as a supporter of Judah, in the east. In the division of Canaan, the tribe of Zebulun was stationed on the west of the Sea of Galilee.

6. Issachar.—Jacob said of Issachar, "He is a strong ass, couching down between two burdens." The emblem inscribed on the banner of Issachar was *a strong ass, couching between two burdens.* The place of Issachar in the desert-encampment was as a supporter of Judah, in the east. In the division of Canaan, the tribe of Issachar was stationed south of Zebulun, on the Plain of Esdrelon.

7. Dan.—Jacob said of Dan, "Dan shall judge his people, as one of the tribes of Israel. Dan shall be a serpent by the way, an adder in the path, that biteth the horse-heels, so that his rider shall fall backward." The emblem inscribed on the banner of Dan was *a serpent biting the heels of a mounted horse.* The place of Dan in the desert-encampment was on the north side, Asher and Naphtali being his supporters. In the division of Canaan, the tribe of Dan was stationed north of Simeon, on the Mediterranean coast.

8. Gad.—Jacob said of Gad, "A troop shall overcome

him, but he shall overcome at the last." The emblem inscribed on the banner of Gad was *a troop of horsemen.* The place of Gad in the desert-encampment was as a supporter of Reuben, in the south. In the division of Canaan, the tribe of Gad was stationed north of Reuben, east of the Jordan.

9. ASHER.—Jacob said of Asher, "Out of Asher his bread shall be fat, and he shall yield royal dainties." The emblem inscribed on the banner of Asher was *a prolific tree.* The place of Asher in the desert-encampment was as a supporter of Dan, in the north. In the division of Canaan, the tribe of Asher was stationed in the north-west, along the Mediterranean coast.

10. NAPHTALI.—Jacob said of Naphtali, "Naphtali is a hind let loose: he giveth goodly words." The emblem inscribed on the banner of Naphtali was *a hind let loose.* The place of Naphtali in the desert-encampment was as a supporter of Dan, in the north. In the division of Canaan, the tribe of Naphtali was stationed in the north.

11. JOSEPH.—Jacob said of Joseph, "Joseph is a fruitful bough, even a fruitful bough by a wall, whose branches run over the wall. His bow abode in strength, and the arms of his hands were made strong by the hands of the mighty God of Jacob. The blessings of thy father shall be on the head of Joseph." The emblem inscribed on the banners of the two sons of Joseph, Ephraim and Manasseh, was *luxuriant branches overrunning a wall.* The place of Ephraim in the desert-encampment was on the west. Manasseh and Benjamin were his supporters. In the division of Canaan, the tribe of Ephraim was stationed north of Benjamin, running from the Jordan to the Mediterranean coast. The

tribe of Manasseh had two portions, one occupying the space between Ephraim and Issachar; the other north of Gad, and extending along the east of the Sea of Galilee to the base of Mount Hermon.

12. BENJAMIN.—Jacob said of Benjamin, "Benjamin shall raven as a wolf; in the morning he shall devour the prey, and at night he shall divide the spoil." The emblem inscribed on the banner of Benjamin was a *ravening wolf.* The place of Benjamin in the desert-encampment was as a supporter of Ephraim, in the west. In the division of Canaan, the tribe of Benjamin was stationed north of Judah.

In the prophecy of Moses, delivered just before his death, (Deut. xxxiii,) he reiterates these blessings, elaborating upon the symbolisms of Jacob, and giving strange beauty to the definitions of these devices.

The groupings of the twelve standards deserve our attention. It will be seen by the sketch we have given, and by an examination of the 10th chapter of Numbers, that the general order of march was as follows:

I. Judah.
Issachar. Zebulun.

II. Reuben.
Simeon. Gad.
Levi.

III. Ephraim.
Manasseh. Benjamin.

IV. Dan.
Asher. Naphtali.

This brings together the banners in groups, thus:

I. Ass, lion, ship.
II. Dagger, young man, troop of horse.
Sword.
III. Fruitful bough, fruitful bough, wolf.
IV. Goodly tree, serpent and horse, bounding hart.

The respective numbers of the twelve tribes thus arrayed for march or battle are thus given, (Num. iii):

I	54,400	74,600	57,400
II	59,300	46,500	45,650
III	32,200	40,500	35,400
IV	41,500	62,700	53,400

THE SILVER TRUMPETS.—The military signals for this grand army were made upon two silver trumpets. These were made of "an whole piece" of metal, and used for the calling of the assembly and for the journeying of the camps.

A certain signal upon *one trumpet* was for the princes, "the heads of the thousands of Israel," to assemble themselves together "at the door of the tabernacle of the congregation."

An alarm blast, blown *once*, was the signal for Judah, Issachar, and Zebulun, who were on the east, to move forward.

An alarm blast, blown *twice*, was the signal for Reuben, Simeon, and Gad, who were on the *south*, to move forward. But when the congregation was to be gathered together, they should blow, but should not sound an alarm. The sons of Aaron, the priests, should blow with the trumpets, and they should be to them "for an ordinance forever, throughout their generations."

LET YOUR LIGHT SHINE

"Let your light shine," the Master said,
To bless benighted man;
The light and truth my Word hath spread,
Are yours to spread again."

We come, O Lord, with willing mind,
That knowledge to display;
Enlighten us, by nature blind,
And gladly we'll obey.

THE VEILS OF THE TABERNACLE.

In the American system of the ROYAL ARCH, great prominence is given to the veils or curtains of the Tabernacle. These are made and set up, as nearly as possible, in imitation of those prepared in the wilderness by direct inspiration from God; also, those afterward constructed under the directions of Solomon, of which the description is, "He made the veil of blue, and purple, and crimson, and fine linen, and wrought cherubim thereon." (2 Chron., iii.)

The Tabernacle, of which the veils or curtains were used as drapery, was built for God, partly to be the palace of his presence as the King of Israel, and partly as the place of the most solemn acts of public worship. It was constructed with extraordinary magnificence in every part, according to the express instruction of Jehovah, and evidently with typical design and use. The means of building it were furnished in superabundance by the voluntary contributions of the people. The oversight of the work was intrusted to Bezaleel and Aholiab, each of whom was endowed with supernatural skill for that purpose, and who bore the same relation to this structure which the Operative Grand Master Hiram bore to the Temple of Solomon. The plan, size, material, furniture, etc., to the most minute particulars, were revealed to Moses upon Mount Sinai. The whole space inclosed for the Tabernacle was one hundred and fifty feet by seventy-five. This space was surrounded by fine linen curtains, nearly eight feet in height, and hung from brazen or copper pillars. They were secured by rods or cords, fastened to the top, and stretched so as to fasten to wooden or metal pins in the ground. Twenty of these pillars or columns were on each side, and ten on each end. The entrance or gate of the court was closed with a curtain of different color and texture from the rest, stretched on four of the pillars, and so hung as to be drawn up or let down at pleasure.

At the upper part or western end of this inclosure, and facing the entrance, was the Tabernacle, properly so called, of which all that we have thus far described was but the fencing. This Tabernacle proper was forty-five by fifteen feet, and fifteen feet high. The sides and rear were inclosed with boards, the front was open. Over the top was thrown a rich, gorgeous fabric, of various materials, the connection and disposition of which, as well as of the other parts of the covering, were prescribed with the utmost minuteness. The entrance or door of the Tabernacle was covered with a beautifully-embroidered curtain, suspended on five columns. The interior was subdivided into two apartments, and separated, each from the other, by a richly-wrought curtain, hanging entirely across, and reaching from the top to the bottom. This was called the veil, or second veil, because the first entrance was also curtained. The outer apartment was called the Holy Place or Sanctuary, or the first Tabernacle, and the inner was the second Tabernacle or the Most Holy Place, or the Holiest of all. The Tabernacle and its court were finished with perfect exactness, according to the pattern or model supernaturally revealed to Moses. And it is estimated that the silver and gold used in its construction, to say nothing of the brass or copper, the wood, the curtains and canopies, the furniture, etc., amounted to an almost incredible sum. When it was finished, it was consecrated, with very solemn and imposing rites, to the service of Jehovah.

As all this was used, with more or less exactness, in the construction of Solomon's Temple, afterward in that by Zerubbabel, of which the Degree of ROYAL ARCH MASON particularly treats, and still later in that by Herod, made forever memorable by the visits of Jesus Christ, a sketch of the use and history of the first Tabernacle is appended:

While passing through the wilderness, the Tabernacle was always pitched in the midst of the camp. The tents of the Levites and priests surrounded it in appointed order, and at some distance from them the residue of the tribes, in four great divisions, consisting of three tribes each, and each division with its appropriate name and standard, or banner. On the east was Judah, assisted by Issachar and Zebulun; on the south Reuben, assisted by Simeon and Gad; on the west Ephraim, assisted by Manasseh and Benjamin; on the north Dan, assisted by Asher and Naphtali. The symbolical banners, relative numbers of the tribes, etc., are minutely given upon another page in this volume.

The Tabernacle and its furniture were so constructed as to be conveniently taken down, transported, and set up again; and particular individuals or classes had their respective duties assigned to them. Every encampment, to the number of forty-two, and every removal, and even the order of the march, were directed expressly by Jehovah. On the day the Tabernacle was completed, God revealed himself in a cloud which overshadowed and filled it. By this cloud assuming the shape of a pillar or column, their subsequent course was governed. When it rested over the tent, the people always rested; and when it moved, the Tabernacle was taken down, and the entire host of Israel followed wherever it led. In the night this cloud became bright, like a pillar of fire, and preceded them in like manner.

When the journeyings of the people ended, and they entered Canaan, the Tabernacle was erected at Gilgal, where it continued until the country was subdued; thence it was removed to Shiloh, where it stood between three hundred and four hundred years. It was thence removed to Nob, and thence, in the reign of David, to Gibeon, where it stood at the commencement of Solomon's reign. When the Temple was finished, the sacred fabric, with its vessels and furniture, described on another page, was removed into it; and there its history is lost.

THE HUMAN BODY A TABERNACLE.—It is a common and beautiful figure of speech, especially in the New Testament, to describe the human body as a tabernacle of clay. One of the Christian poets carries the allegory to a charming point when he describes the pious man as nightly pitching his tent

"A day's march nearer home."

In the same spirit the following lines have been composed:

The Craft, in days gone by,
Drew from their mystery
The mightiest truths God ever gave to men;
They whispered in the ear
Bowed down with solemn fear,
"The dead, the buried dead, shall live again!"

O wondrous, wondrous Word!
No other rites afford
This precious heritage, this matchless truth;
Though gone from weeping eyes,
Though in the dust he lies,
Our friend, our brother, shall renew his youth.

And we who yet remain,
Shall meet our dead again—
Shall give the hand that thrilled within our grasp
The token of our faith,
Unchanged by time and death,
And breast to breast his faithful form shall clasp.

But who, O gracious God,
The power shall afford?
Who, with omnipotence, shall break the tomb?
What Morning Star shall rise
To chase from sealêd eyes
The long-oppressing darkness and the gloom?

Lo! at the mystic shrine
The answer—'tis Divine;
Lo! where the tracing-board doth plainly tell:

"Over the horrid tomb,
Its bondage and its gloom,
The Lion of the Tribe of Judah shall prevail!"

Then hopefully we bend
Above our sleeping friend,
And, hopeful, cast the green sprigs o'er his head;
'T is but a fleeting hour—
The Omnipotent hath power,
And He will raise our brother from the dead.

THE ALTAR.

The use of the Altar in the ceremonies of the ROYAL ARCH is even more impressive than in other grades. Under the Jewish law, an altar was a structure appropriated exclusively to the offering of sacrifices. Though sacrifices were offered before the Flood, the word altar does not occur until the time of Noah's departure from the Ark.

Altars were of various forms, and at first very rude in their construction, being nothing more, probably, than a square heap of stones or a mound of earth. The altar upon which Jacob made an offering at Bethel was the single stone which had served him for a pillow during the night. The altar which Moses was commanded to build was to be made of earth; or, if made of stone, it was expressly required to be rough, the use of a tool being regarded as polluting. It was also to be without steps.

In the ancient patterns of altars, although the structures are different, yet we observe upon the most of them a projection upward at each corner, representing the true figure of *the horns*, used, probably, to confine the victims. This should be imitated upon the Masonic Altar.

The altars required in the Jewish worship, from which so much of the allegory of the ROYAL ARCH is borrowed, were the *Altar of Burnt-offering*, or the Brazen Altar, and the *Altar of Incense*, or the Golden Altar. The first stood directly in front of the principal entrance of the Tabernacle in the wilderness. It was made of shittim-wood, which is doubtless the Masonic Acacia, one of the finest emblems upon the Trestle-board of Freemasonry. It was seven feet six inches square, and four feet six inches high. It was hollow, and covered or overlaid with plates of brass. The horns upon each corner were of wood, overlaid in the same way. A grate or net-work of brass was also attached to it, either to hold the fire or to support a hearth of earth. The furniture of the altar was all of brass, and consisted of a shovel, a pan, skins or vessels for receiving the blood of the victims, and hooks for turning the sacrifice. At each corner of the altar was a brass ring, and there were also two staves or rods, overlaid with brass, which passed through these rings, and served for carrying the altar from place to place.

The fire used upon this altar was divinely sent and perpetually maintained. The altar was a place of constant sacrifice; fresh blood was shed upon it continually, and the smoke of the burning sacrifice ascended up without interruption toward heaven. In the first Temple the Altar of Burnt-offering occupied the same relative position as in the Tabernacle: it was thirty feet square, and fifteen feet high. In the Temple of Zerubbabel it was still larger and more beautiful than in the first.

The Altar of Incense stood within the Holy Place, near the inmost veil. It was eighteen inches square, and twice as high, constructed like the other. The top, sides, and horns were overlaid with pure gold, and it was finished around the upper surface with a crown or border. The rings and rods were like the other, gold being used instead of brass. Incense was burned every morning and evening upon it, but no other offerings. Only once a year, when the Priest made atonement, was it stained with blood.

THE BURNING BUSH.

There are few incidents in the early Scriptures more remarkable or significant than that in which the emblem of the Burning Bush figures. It is described in the third chapter of Exodus:

"Now Moses kept the flock of Jethro his father-in-law, the priest of Midian: and he led the flock to the back side of the desert, and came to the mountain of God, even to Horeb.

"And the angel of the Lord appeared unto him in a flame of fire out of the midst of a bush: and he looked, and behold, the bush burned with fire, and the bush was not consumed.

"And Moses said, I will now turn aside, and see this great sight, why the bush is not burnt.

"And when the Lord saw that he turned aside to see, God called unto him out of the midst of the bush, and said, Moses, Moses. And he said, Here am I.

"And he said, Draw not nigh hither: put off thy

shoes from off thy feet, for the place whereon thou standest is holy ground.

"Moreover he said, I am the God of thy father, the God of Abraham, the God of Isaac, and the God of Jacob. And Moses hid his face: for he was afraid to look upon God."

This remarkable display of Omnipotent power was the preamble to a most important declaration to Moses; viz., that God had looked with a pitying eye upon the sorrows of his people, bondsmen in Egypt; that the time of their deliverance was now nigh at hand, and that he, Moses, was the chosen instrument in the hand of God to bring them forth from slavery.

Perhaps the ineffable brightness of the Godhead was never so clearly poured upon mortal vision as in that memorable transaction which this symbol is designed to signify. We know that "no man can see God face to face and live;" therefore the prophet hid his face, unable to sustain the bright effulgence of uncreated glory. It is but a natural deduction, from this circumstance, to teach that, in order to gain admission into the heavenly mount, burning with far greater brilliancy than that which dazzled the wanderer on the back side of the desert, we must be purified by fire.

As this was the beginning of the career of Moses as the Lawgiver and Leader of the hosts of Israel, it will be proper to add that the history of his official life for the forty years following is the history of the Jewish nation from the close of their bondage in Egypt to their approach to the land of promise. The miracles God wrought by his hands; his frequent opportunities of communing immediately with the Divine Majesty; the wonderful displays he witnessed of the power and glory of Jehovah, and his connection with the grand and significant system of religious rites and ceremonies, which is called after him *the Mosaic ritual or dispensation;* the severity of the rebukes he suffered in consequence of a single sinful act; his extraordinary meekness; the singular manner of his death; and the fact that he is the historian of ages and events so remote and so intensely interesting to us in our various relations, prospects, and circumstances, all combine to make him, perhaps, the most extraordinary man that ever lived.

There is one use to be made of the Burning Bush as an emblem, too direct and striking to be overlooked. As this Bush, although on fire, was not consumed, so the Church of God, and, in the same allegory, the Masonic institution, though, from age to age, burning under the fires of persecution, have never been consumed. Nor can they be. God is in them—"the God of Abraham, and the God of Isaac, and the God of Jacob"—and they can not be consumed. In the Masons' Lodge *His Word* lies open, the center of attraction, the object to which all entering must approach. In the east of the Lodge, *His initial* shines forth, catching the eye of one entering when he raises it from the open Word. *His name* is ever invoked in prayers, covenants, lectures, instructions. This Bush, though burning, can never be consumed while God is in it.

Too much can not be written to impress on the minds of members of the Masonic institution, that without this theory of the continued presence of God in the meetings of the Craft, the whole structure, so elaborately constructed by the fathers, and cemented from age to age by the devotion of the members, must fall to the ground. Without this theory, much of the emblems and other instructions are without meaning. The following lines, written for the consecration service of a Masonic body, are appropriate here:

Lo, God is here! our prayers prevail;
In deeper reverence adore;
Ask freely now, he will not fail
His largest, richest gifts to pour.

Ask by these emblems, old and true;
Ask by the memories of the past;
Ask by his own great name, for, lo,
His every promise there is cast!

Ask WISDOM, 'tis the chiefest thing;
Ask STRENGTH, such strength as God may yield;
Ask BEAUTY from his throne to spring,
And grace the temple as we build.

Lord God most High, our Lodge we veil!
'T is consecrate with ancient care;
O, let thy Spirit ever dwell,
And guide the loving builders here!

THE UNITY OF FREEMASONS.

In close connection with the above remarks, follow those upon the unity of the Craft. This is an immediate effect of the presence of God in the Burning Bush. The following comment upon the 133d Psalm, so wonderfully adapted to Masonic use in every grade, is appended as he best effort of the sort extant:

"We see in verse 1 what it is we are commanded; viz., *to dwell together in unity*. Not only not to quarrel and devour each other, but to delight in each other with mutual endearments, and promote each other's welfare with mutual services. See, also, how commendable it is: 'Behold, how good and how pleasant it is.' Good in itself, because agreeable to God's will—the conformity of earth to heaven. Good for us, for our honor and comfort; pleasant and pleasing to God and good men. A rare thing, and therefore commendable. An amiable thing, that will attract our hearts. An exemplary thing, which, where it is, is to be imitated by us with holy emulation.

"The pleasantness of it is illustrated in verse 2. It is fragrant as the holy anointing oil which was strongly perfumed, and diffused its odors, to the great delight of all the bystanders, when it was poured upon the head of Aaron or his successor, the high-priest, so plentifully that it ran down the face, even to the collar or binding of the garment. This was *holy* ointment; such must our brotherly love be with a pure heart devoted to God. We must love them that are begotten 'for His sake that begat.' This ointment was a composition made up by a Divine dispensatory. God appointed the ingredients and the quantities. Thus believers are 'taught of God to love one another.' It is a grace of His working in us.

"It was *very precious*, and the like of it was not to be made for any common use. Thus holy love is, in the sight of God, of great price; and that is precious indeed which is so in God's sight. It was grateful both to Aaron himself and to all about him. So is holy love;

it is like 'ointment and perfume which rejoice the heart.' Aaron and his sons were not admitted to minister unto the Lord till they were anointed with this ointment; nor are our services acceptable to God without this holy love. If we have it not, we are nothing.

"It is said in the third verse to be fructifying. It is profitable as well as pleasing. It is 'as the dew;' it brings abundance of blessings along with it, as numerous as the drops of dew. It cools the scorching heat of men's passions as the evening dews cool the air and refresh the earth. It contributes very much to our fruitfulness in every thing that is good. It moistens the heart, and makes it tender and fit to receive the good seed of the Word; as, on the contrary, malice and bitterness unfit us to receive it. It is 'as the dew of Hermon,' a *common hill;* for brotherly love is the beauty and benefit of civil societies; 'and as the dew that descended upon the mountains of Zion,' a *holy hill*, for it contributes greatly to the fruitfulness of sacred societies. Both Hermon and Zion will wither without this dew. It is said of the dew, 'that it tarrieth not for man, nor waiteth for the sons of men.' Nor should our love for our brethren stay for theirs to us—that is *publican's love*—but go before it; that is *Divine love*.

"The proof of the excellency of brotherly love is given in the fourth verse. Loving people are blessed people; for they are blessed of God, and therefore blessed indeed. There where brethren dwell together in unity the Lord commands the blessing, a complicated blessing, including all blessings. It is God's prerogative to *command* the blessings; man can but *beg* a blessing. Blessings, according to the promise, are commanded blessings, for

He has 'commanded His covenant forever.' Blessings that take effect are commanded blessings, for 'He speaks, and it is done.'

"They are everlastingly blessed. The blessing which God commands on them that dwell in love is 'life for evermore;' that is the blessing of blessings. They that dwell in love not only dwell in God, but do already dwell in heaven. As the perfection of love is the blessedness of heaven, so the sincerity of love is the earnest of that blessedness. They that live in love and peace, shall have the God of love and peace with them now, and they shall be with him shortly, with him forever, in the world of love and peace. How good, then, it is, and how pleasant!"

THE LAND OF PALESTINE.

All the localities described in the Masonic lectures are connected with Palestine or the countries—Egypt and Chaldea—contiguous thereto. This makes it necessary, in a course of instruction like this, to give a sketch of what is familiarly termed "the Holy Land."

The extreme length of the country, measured from Dan to Beersheba, is about one hundred and eighty miles. Its average breadth is fifty, from the Mediterranean Sea to the deserts on the east. The area of the country is not far from twelve thousand miles, which is about the size of Vermont, to which State it also approximates in shape and ruggedness.

There is no district on the face of the earth that contains so many and such sudden transitions as Palestine. It is at once a land of mountains, plains, and valleys.

In the north, the Lebanon Mountains divide into two parallel ranges. The western range has summits of thirteen thousand feet. It is broken by the River Leontes, opposite Tyre; decreases in height but expands in breadth to Nazareth, where it is again broken by the Plain of Esdrælon. Rising again into the hills of Samaria, this range continues thirty-three miles, and is, for the third time, broken by the Plain of Shechem, near Mount Gerizim. Rising again into the hills of Ephraim, of Benjamin, and of Judah, it finally terminates in the deserts to the south.

The eastern range includes Mount Hermon, ten thousand feet high; sweeps from thence round the Sea of Galilee eastward into the mountains of Bashan, Gilead, Ammon, Moab, and Edom, and terminates in the hills of Arabia Petrea, at the head of the Bay of Akabah. These two parallel ranges, covering, as they do, four-fifths of the whole country, form the most prominent features in Palestine. The valley that separates them, called Cœlesyria, is three hundred and fifty miles in length, and from seven to ten miles broad, serving as the bed of the Orontes, the Litany, and the Jordan.

The greater portion of the towns and cities of Palestine were situated in the hilly country. This was for protection, in a country always subject to invasion. Jerusalem, Bethlehem, Hebron, Bethel, Shiloh, and Samaria are instances of this.

Although at present Palestine is but thinly inhabited, its soil poorly cultivated, and the state of society uncivilized in the extreme, yet, in the days when the name and the law of God were respected, this was one of the most populous, civilized, and fruitful nations upon earth.

There is almost an air of extravagance in the inspired description of Palestine. Its marvelous richness; its cattle upon a thousand hills; its metallic wealth; its abounding pastures; its people, numerous, strong, and respected throughout the earth, all these combined to make it the chosen nation of the world. The hills were terraced to their very tops for purposes of cultivation. The numerous springs and fountains were used to irrigate, to the last drop, the soil around. The rains of heaven were collected in great pools and cisterns, of which the remains every-where attract the eye to the present day. And, under the guidance of the wisest sages, the arts of agriculture, commerce, and architecture made Palestine a coveted land, ages before Greece and Rome sprung from obscurity.

Such was the beautiful territory from which the people, consequent upon their conquest by Nebuchadnezzar, were banished, to become exiles in an unfriendly land. The story of their calamity is a sad one. Divided into two nations, under Rehoboam, B. C. 971, the national power and reputation of Israel were henceforth diminished by internecine wars. Shishak, King of Egypt, invaded the country only four years after the death of Solomon, captured Jerusalem, and plundered the Temple. One hundred and forty-five years afterward, the northern tribes invaded the southern, captured Jerusalem, and inflicted great destruction upon it. From these misfortunes, however, Judah had recovered, when, in the year B. C. 588, Nebuchadnezzar, King of Babylon, assisted by all the surrounding nations, who were his tributaries, brought overwhelming numbers against Judah, and it succumbed. The Scriptural account is as follows:

"Jehoiakim was twenty and five years old when he began to reign, and he reigned eleven years in Jerusalem: and he did that which was *evil* in the sight of the Lord his God.

"Against him came up Nebuchadnezzar, King of Babylon, and bound him in fetters, to carry him to Babylon.

"Nebuchadnezzar also carried off the vessels of the house of the Lord to Babylon, and put them in his temple at Babylon.

"Jehoiachin was eight years old when he began to reign, and he reigned three months and ten days in Jerusalem: and he did that which was *evil* in the sight of the Lord.

"And King Nebuchadnezzar sent and brought him to Babylon, with the goodly vessels of the house of the Lord, and made Zedekiah his brother king over Judah and Jerusalem,

"Zedekiah was one and twenty years old when he began to reign, and reigned eleven years in Jerusalem.

"And he did that which was *evil* in the sight of the Lord his God, and humbled not himself before Jeremiah the prophet speaking from the mouth of the Lord.

"And he also rebelled against King Nebuchadnezzar, who *had made him swear by God:* but he stiffened his neck, and hardened his heart from turning unto the Lord God of Israel.

"Moreover all the chief of the priests, and the people, transgressed very much after all the abominations of the heathen; and polluted the house of the Lord which he had hallowed in Jerusalem.

"And the Lord God of their fathers sent to them by

his messengers, rising up betimes, and sending; because he had compassion on his people, and on his dwelling-place:

"But they mocked the messengers of God, and despised his words, and misused his prophets, until the wrath of the Lord arose against his people, *till there was no remedy.*

"Therefore he brought upon them the King of the Chaldees, who slew their young men with the sword in the house of their sanctuary, and had no compassion upon young man or maiden, old man, or him that stooped for age: he gave them all into his hand.

"And all the vessels of the house of God, great and small, and the treasures of the house of the king and of his princes; all these he brought to Babylon.

"And they burnt the house of God, and brake down the wall of Jerusalem, and burnt all the palaces thereof with fire, and destroyed all the goodly vessels thereof.

"All them that had escaped from the sword carried he away to Babylon; where they were servants to him and to his sons, until the reign of the kingdom of Persia:

"To fulfill the word of the Lord by the mouth of Jeremiah, until the land had enjoyed her sabbaths: for as long as she lay desolate she kept sabbath, to fulfill threescore and ten years."—2 Chron., xxxvi.

In the 2d Book of Kings, further particulars of this terrible and crushing calamity are given. The siege of Jerusalem lasted eighteen months:

"The famine prevailed in the city, and there was no bread for the people of the land.

"And the city was broken up, and all the men of war fled by night by the way of the gate between two walls, which is by the king's garden: and the king (Zedekiah) went the way toward the plain (of Jericho).

"And the army of the Chaldees pursued after the king, and overtook him in the plains of Jericho: and all his army were scattered from him.

"So they took the king, and brought him up to the king of Babylon to Riblah; and they gave judgment upon him.

"And they slew the sons of Zedekiah before his eyes, and put out the eyes of Zedekiah, and bound him with fetters of brass, and carried him to Babylon."

The great pillars, Jachin and Boaz, which stood eastward from the Temple, were broken in pieces, and carried to Babylon; the better portion of the people taken into exile, and the poor of the land only left to be vine-dressers and husbandmen. Thus lay the Holy Land—the kingdom extinct, the country wasted, the fenced cities dismantled, and the nation in captivity. A provincial government was established, under the Babylonish government. This event occurred four hundred and sixty-eight years after David began to reign in Hebron, three hundred and eighty-eight years after the revolt of the ten tribes under Rehoboam, and one hundred and thirty-four years after the downfall of the rival nation thus formed.

The journey of the exiles to Babylon was, upon some accounts, the most pathetic event recorded in the annals of history. The distance, upon a direct line, was but six hundred miles, but taking the journey, extended by the necessity of water, fuel, and forage, it was not less than eight hundred. From Jerusalem, through Bethel and Shiloh, forty miles to Samaria, was a hilly region, hard, indeed, to the bare and lacerated feet of princes, rulers, delicate females, and old age. A short rest in the fertile plains of Samaria, and then another hilly region of thirty miles was interposed to the beautiful plain of Esdrælon, the richest and most fertile in Palestine—the scene of the national glories under Barak, Gideon, and other mighty men of Israel. Another more painful pilgrimage, of one hundred miles and upward followed, to the region of Damascus. Then began the desert, arid, torrid, and solitary. A long stretch of this, during which thousands of the captives, doubtless, left their bones by the wayside, brought the exiles to Palmyra, or Tadmor in the Wilderness. This splendid resting-place in the desert was their last reminder of the Jewish King Solomon, its builder.

From Palmyra, over the almost interminable deserts, to the river Euphrates, and now the bitterness of their journey began to be assuaged. The comforts of life were more freely bestowed; more attention was given to the little ones, and to the sick. Their conquerors apportioned them off, according to rules of consanguinity, in the fertile tracts and flourishing towns of Chaldea. God did not forsake his people in those distant parts. Prophets, such as Daniel and Ezekiel, gave them comfortable hopes of pardon and release. Esther, one of their kindred, was made queen, and they received great benefits from her royal favor. In fact, their condition was one of comparative honor and comfort. By many stupendous miracles, their God became known and feared throughout the empire, and by important services rendered to the state by those Jews who held high offices, the royal favor was the more readily moved toward the nation. Their idolatry, which had been marked by the Divine eye as the worst of the long catalogue of their offenses, was effectually cured, and whatever faults the Jews may have committed after their release from captivity, during the remainder of their existence as a nation, that of idolatry can not be charged against them. In our next chapter we describe their return to Jerusalem.

THE RETURN HOME.

In the forty-ninth year from the destruction of Jerusalem, and the sixty-seventh year of the captivity, in the year B. C. 539, the Babylonish monarchy was overthrown by Cyrus, the young prince of Persia, commander of the combined forces of the Medes and Persians. His uncle, Darius, took the kingdom and thus founded the Medo-Persian Empire, as foretold by the Prophet Daniel. The Babylonian Empire had existed eighty-four years, having been founded B. C. 623. Darius lived but two years after the establishment of his power in Babylon, dying in the sixty-ninth year of the captivity. He was succeeded by Cyrus. This man had been distinctly mentioned by name in the prophecy of Isaiah, made and recorded more than a hundred years before he was born. It had been predicted of him that he should both overthrow the Babylonish monarchy and restore the Jews to their native land and their former privileges.

In the first year of the reign of Cyrus and the seventieth of the captivity, he issued a proclamation throughout his empire, granting a release to all the Jewish captives, with full privileges to return to Palestine, rebuild Jerusalem, and resuscitate the nation. At the same time he restored all the sacred vessels of the Temple, which had been carried away by Nebuchadnezzar, and made other provisions for the immediate accomplishment of the objects of the royal edict.

THE FIFTEEN STAGES OF THE RETURN JOURNEY.—It is a Rabbinical tradition, that on the return journey the people made fifteen prominent stages, each being terminated by a halt of sufficient duration for rest and refreshment: and that the short Psalms, from 120 to 134, inclusive, were sung respectively upon those occasions. The First Stage opens with the expression, "In my distress I cried unto the Lord;" the Second Stage, by this, "I will lift up mine eyes unto the hills from whence cometh my help;" the Third Stage, "I was glad when they said unto me, Let us go unto the house of the Lord;" the Fourth Stage, "Unto Thee lift I up mine eyes, O Thou that dwellest in the heavens;" the Fifth Stage, "If it had not been for the Lord, who was on our side;" the Sixth Stage, "They that trust in the Lord, shall be as Mount Zion, which can not be removed, but abideth forever;" the Seventh Stage, "When the Lord turned again the captivity of Zion, we were like them that dream;" the Eighth Stage, "Except the Lord build the house, they labor in vain that build it;" the Ninth Stage, "Blessed is every one that feareth the Lord, that walketh in his ways;" the Tenth Stage, "Many a time have they afflicted me from my youth, may Israel now say;" the Eleventh Stage, "Out of the deptns have I cried unto Thee, O Lord;" the Twelfth Stage, "Lord, my heart is not haughty, nor my eyes lofty;" the Thirteenth Stage, "Lord, remember David and all his afflictions;" the Fourteenth Stage, "Behold how good and pleasant it is for brethren to dwell together in unity;" the Fifteenth and last Stage, "Behold, bless ye the Lord, all ye servants of the Lord, which by night stand in the house of the Lord."

Before following the Jews from the place of their long exile in Chaldea, it is proper here to quote the whole of the 137th Psalm, as giving evidence of their commendable constancy amidst the most untoward circumstances:

"By the rivers of Babylon, there we sat down; yea, we wept, when we remembered Zion.

"We hanged our harps upon the willows in the midst thereof.

"For there they that carried us away captive required of us a song; and they that wasted us required of us mirth, saying, Sing us one of the songs of Zion.

"How shall we sing the Lord's song in a strange land?

"If I forget thee, O Jerusalem, let my right hand forget her cunning.

"If I do not remember thee, let my tongue cleave to the roof of my mouth; if I prefer not Jerusalem above my chief joy.

"Remember, O Lord, the children of Edom in the day of Jerusalem; who said, Rase it, rase it, even to the foundation thereof.

"O daughter of Babylon, who art to be destroyed;

happy shall he be that rewardeth thee as thou hast served us.

"Happy shall he be that taketh and dasheth thy little ones against the stones."

THE NATIONAL BEREAVEMENT.—The excessive sorrow that afflicted the minds of the Jews at the loss of their country can not be thoroughly appreciated, unless we take into consideration the facts that these people had possessed Palestine for twelve hundred years, counting from the entrance of Abraham; that their religious polity was thoroughly identified with it, and that their hopes of the Messiah, who should restore to the world all that had been lost in the expulsion from Eden, were locally connected with Bethlehem-Judah, and other designated spots. The lamentations of which the Prophet Jeremiah was the mouthpiece are not an extravagant expression of the national sorrow. Although uttered only as predictions, they foreshadowed the grievous facts that should follow. In this terrible exhibit of human distress we find such passages as these:

"How doth the city sit solitary that was full of people! how is she become as a widow! She weepeth sore in the night, and her tears are in her cheeks. All her friends have dealt treacherously with her; they are become her enemies. She dwelleth among the heathen, she findeth no rest. Her children are gone into captivity before the enemy. From the daughter of Zion all her beauty is departed. Jerusalem hath grievously sinned; therefore she is removed. All her people sigh;

they seek bread. See if there be any sorrow like unto my sorrow. The Lord hath trodden under foot all my mighty men in the midst of thee.

"The Lord hath purposed to destroy the wall of the daughter of Zion; he hath stretched out a line, he hath not withdrawn his hand from destroying. The elders of the daughter of Zion sit upon the ground and keep silence. The children and the sucklings swoon in the streets of the city. They say to their mothers, Where is corn and wine? All that pass by, clap their hands at thee; they hiss and wag their head at the daughter of Jerusalem, saying, Is this the city that men call The Perfection of beauty, The Joy of the whole earth? The tongue of the sucking child cleaveth to the roof of his mouth for thirst; the young children ask bread, and no man breaketh it unto them. The punishment of the iniquity of the daughter of my people is greater than the punishment of the sin of Sodom. They that be slain with the sword are better than they that be slain with hunger.

"Our inheritance is turned to strangers, our houses to aliens. We are orphans and fatherless, our mothers are as widows. Our necks are under persecution: we labor, and have no rest. Our skin was black as an oven because of the terrible famine. They ravished the women in Zion, and the maids in the cities of Judah. Princes are hanged up by their hand: the faces of elders were not honored. The joy of our heart is ceased; our dance is turned into mourning. The crown is fallen from our head. O Lord, thou hast utterly rejected us; thou art very wroth against us."—Lamentations.

In vivid contrast with this condition of humiliation and distress was the national joy that broke forth upon the proclamation of Cyrus, to which the Lord stirred up his spirit. It was in these words:

"Thus saith Cyrus king of Persia, The Lord God of heaven hath given me all the kingdoms of the earth; and he hath charged me to build him an house at Jerusalem, which is in Judah. Who is there among you of all his people? his God be with him, and let him go up to Jerusalem, which is in Judah, and build the house of the Lord God of Israel, (he is the God,) which is in Jerusalem. And whosoever remaineth in any place where he sojourneth, let the men of his place help him with silver, and with gold, and with goods, and with beasts, besides the free-will offering for the house of God which is in Jerusalem."—Ezra, i.

An expedition of the returning exiles was formed by Zerubbabel, a descendant of the royal house of David, and by Joshua, the high-priest. Zerubbabel was invested by the king with all the functions of the Governor of Judea. This colony amounted to about fifty thousand persons. These took with them the vessels of the house of the Lord, being "thirty chargers of gold, a thousand chargers of silver, nine and twenty knives, thirty basins of gold, silver basins of a second sort, four hundred and ten, and other vessels a thousand. All the vessels of gold and silver were five thousand and four hundred." (Ezra, i.) The Jews, who for various reasons remained behind, strengthened the hands of their rude, zealous friends with "money, goods, beasts, and precious things, besides, all that was willingly offered." This made the caravan to include seven hundred and thirty-six horses, two hundred and forty-five mules, four hundred and thirty-five camels, and six thousand seven hundred and twenty asses. The money contributed by the more liberal of the Jews is summed up at sixty-one thousand drams of gold, and five thousand pounds of silver.

So, joyfully they set forth upon the return journey by the same route which their sorrowing and suffering fathers had traveled fifty-one years before. Arrived at Palestine, their first care, after looking up their former homes, and making necessary provisions for their future support, was to rebuild the Temple. In the second year of their coming, Zerubbabel and Joshua, who had taken the supervision, set forward the workmen in the house of God.

"And when the builders laid the foundation of the Temple of the Lord, they set the priests in their apparel, (described upon another page,) with trumpets, and the Levites the sons of Asaph with cymbals, to praise the Lord after the ordinance of David king of Israel. And they sang together by course in praising and giving thanks unto the Lord; because he is good, for his mercy endureth forever toward Israel. And all the people shouted with a great shout, when they praised the Lord, because the foundation of the house of the Lord was laid. But many of the priests and Levites, and chief of the fathers, who were ancient men, that had seen the first house, when the foundation of this house was laid before their eyes, wept with a loud voice; and many shouted aloud for joy: so that the people could not discern the noise of the shout of joy from the noise of the weeping of the people: for the people shouted with a loud shout, and the noise was heard afar off."—Ezra, iii.

With all this favorable beginning, however, it was nineteen years before the cape-stone was set in the edifice. The Samaritans, between whom and the Jews there had long existed an implacable hatred, weakened their hands, troubled them in building, and hired counselors against them to frustrate their purpose, through the reign of Cyrus and his successors to that of Darius. Ahasuerus was moved by their malicious representations to cause the building to cease, nor was it until the second year of the reign of Darius that it was resumed. That monarch decreed that no more hindrance should be made to the work, but that money should be given from the royal treasury toward the cost, and young bullocks, rams, and lambs for the burnt-offerings: also wheat, salt, wine, and oil. The royal edict was thus summed up:

Whosoever shall alter this word, let timber be pulled down from his house, and being set up, let him be hanged thereon; and let his house be made a dunghill for this. And the God that hath caused his name to dwell there destroy all kings and people, that shall put to their hand to alter and to destroy this house of God which is at Jerusalem. I Darius have made this decree; let it be done with speed."—Ezra, vi.

RETURNED HOME.

Upon the last page is described the earnestness with which the Jews acted upon the proclamation of Cyrus. A similar zeal was aroused by the edict of Darius. To encourage them in their work, the prophets Haggai and Zechariah were raised up. They approached them in the name of the God of Israel. The former severely rebuked the disposition of the people to lie supine under the frowns of King Ahasuerus, and commanded them, "Go up to the mountain, and bring wood, and build the house," promising them the Divine aid. "I will fill this house with glory, saith the Lord of hosts. The glory of this latter house shall be greater than that of the former."

Zechariah brought good word, and comfortable word from God, saying:

"I am returned to Jerusalem with mercies; mine house shall be built in it; my cities, through prosperity, shall yet be spread abroad, and the Lord shall yet comfort Zion, and shall yet choose Jerusalem.

"The hands of Zerubbabel have laid the foundations of this house; his hands shall also finish it.

"They that are far off shall come, and build in the temple of the Lord: and ye shall know that the Lord of hosts hath sent me unto you. And this shall come to pass if ye will diligently obey the voice of the Lord your God."

A second installment of Jews from Babylon came up, under the command of Ezra, seventy-seven years after the first. Ezra came with full powers from the king to reëstablish the authority of the law of Moses. This second colony numbered about seven thousand. The journey occupied exactly four months, by which we can estimate the difficulties and impediments of the way, even under favorable circumstances.

The king, Artaxerxes Longimanus, issued an edict, exceedingly liberal in its character, and ending in these impressive words:

"And whosoever will not do the law of thy God, and the law of the king, let judgment be executed speedily upon him, whether it be unto death, or to banishment, or to confiscation of goods, or to imprisonment."—Ezra, vii.

Thirteen years later, B. C. 444, the third installment of the nation came up, under Nehemiah. He had received intelligence at Babylon of the decline of the Jewish colony, and obtained a commission from the same monarch, Artaxerxes Longimanus, who had favored Ezra, to visit Jerusalem and rectify the disordered state of affairs. The walls of the city had not been rebuilt, and although the temple was finished, and probably walled in, yet the undefended condition of the people at large subjected them to great reproach and persecution from surrounding nations, the Samaritans taking the lead. Nehemiah was appointed governor for twelve years, with full powers to rebuild the city and restore the ancient fortifications. His arrival was one hundred and twelve years subsequent to that of Zerubbabel. At the expiration of the term of his first commission, he was reappointed, and continued to serve in that capacity until about the year B. C. 420. During the latter years of his government lived Malachi, the last of the Old Testament prophets. Besides these three principal colonies that returned from Babylon to repeople the land, whose loss they had so grievously deplored, we may justly suppose that many thousands of Jews took the opportunity to return to their fatherland by caravans of merchants coming from the east, or in other smaller companies of returning Jews.

The Jewish nation continued subject to the Persian power until its overthrow by Alexander, the Macedonian, B. C. 331. In all, they had maintained their allegiance to Persia two hundred and eight years. In the division of Alexander's empire, Palestine fell to Ptolemy Lagus. They were subject to the Greek-Egyptian and the Greek-Syrian monarchs one hundred and fifty-eight years, and until the year B. C. 143. Then they regained their independence by virtue of a royal grant from Demetrius Nicator, king of the Greek-Syrian empire, and held it eighty years; viz., till the year B. C. 63, when Judea was made a Roman province by Pompey. They were still, however, permitted to have governors of their own nation until the time of Christ. In the year A. D. 9, a Roman governor was appointed, tribute was paid directly to Rome, the power of life and death was taken away, and justice administered in the name and by the laws of Rome. Jerusalem ceased to be the capital of Palestine. In the year A. D. 70, the city of Jerusalem was once more totally razed to the ground by Titus, the Roman general, after a siege and series of assaults, in which more than a million of Jews perished. From this stroke the nation has never recovered. Scattered throughout the earth, exiles, down-trodden, suffered to live in small numbers at Jerusalem, but to enjoy no naturalization or political rights, the Jewish people remain standing monuments of the truth of Scripture. The importance of the study of these holy books to the ROYAL ARCH MASON can not be exaggerated.

O, *early* search the Scriptures! 't is the dew
On morning leaves; 't is the young rose's bloom;
'T is the bright tinge of morning; 't is the hue
That doth on cheek of conscious virtue come;
'T is all that gratifies the sight,
To see this sacred Book aright.

O, *fondly* search the Scriptures! 't is the voice
Of loved ones gone forever; 't is the song
That calls to memory childhood's perished joys
'T is the blest anthem of the angel-throng;
'T is all that gratifies the ear,
This sacred Book aright to hear.

O, *deeply* search the Scriptures! 't is the mine
Of purest gold and gems of richest sort;
'T is life's full sustenance of corn and wine;
'T is raiment, clean and white, from heaven brought;
'T is wealth beyond all we can crave,
This sacred Book aright to have.

For here, O here, the loved departed!
The Man of Sorrows, slain for us,
Speaks to the worn and broken-hearted,
And tells us, "I have borne the curse!
Redeemed thee from the power of death,
And sanctified thy parting breath."

That in bright worlds, depictured here,
Are "many mansions," ample room,

Where Christ our Savior waits to cheer,
And bid us welcome from the tomb:
Where many a friend we counted lost,
Is singing with the heavenly host.

This is the one, the appointed way,
Through which the Holy Ghost doth speak;
O, walk therein, through life's brief day,
And treasures of salvation seek;
Assured there is no other ford
Through Jordan's billows save THE WORD.

THE CITY OF JERUSALEM.

Jerusalem! the City of Peace! Zion! the perfection of beauty! the joy of the whole earth! the City of David! the central point of sacred history, around which revolve all that is historical, all that is symbolical, all that is solemn, grand, or pathetic in the dealings of God with men. The Holy Place! the type of a heavenly city, upon whose eternal glories Ezekiel, Daniel, and John have exhausted their descriptive powers!

Jerusalem! how vividly comes over the mind the memory of that fine old hymn, one of the old-est in our language, one of the finest in any language:

Jerusalem! my happy home!
O, how I long for thee!
When shall my sorrows have an end?
Thy joys when shall I see?

This was the capital of the Jewish kingdom for eleven hundred years. It was the scene of the most extraordinary events that have occurred in the annals of the human race—events in which men and angels have, and must forever have, the deepest interest. It was the place selected by the Almighty for his earthly dwelling, and here his glory was rendered visible. Here David sat and tuned his harp, and sung the praises of Jehovah. Hither the tribes came up, the tribes of the Lord, unto the testimony of Israel, to give thanks unto the name of the Lord. Here enraptured prophets saw bright visions of the world above, and received messages from on high for guilty men. Here our Lord and Savior came in the form of a servant, and groaned and wept, and poured out his soul even unto death, to redeem us from sin, and to save us from the pains of hell. Here, too, the wrath of an incensed God has fallen upon his chosen people, and has laid waste his heritage.

No place upon earth has such a history. For three thousand five hundred years the hills round about Jerusalem have been the scene of mortal strife. The echoes of these mountains have resounded to the war-cries of a hundred nations. Seventeen times has the city been destroyed, and as often rebuilt—now a place of luxury and grandeur, and now a place of silence and desolation.

It was here that Melchizedek met and welcomed the patriarch as he was returning from the defeat of the four kings, at Hobah. Here Abraham returned, forty-two years afterward, upon a mission the most pathetic that can affect a parent's heart. Here David reared an altar when the plague was stayed. And here, as the crowning glory of all, was reared the Sacred Fane, which is equally the object of interest to Royal Arch as to all other classes of Freemasons.

PASSING THE VEILS.

One of the most forcible and instructive lessons in the whole Masonic system is that inculcated in the drama of the ROYAL ARCH DEGREE, under the general term of "Returning from Babylon to Jerusalem." Under the guise of a difficult and painful pilgrimage, in which the travelers are buoyed up by the sense of duty and the hope of reward, the whole lesson of human life is conveyed, surrounded with trials and perplexities, but presenting the highest injunctions of duty as a stimulus, and offering the most exalted rewards at the end. It is this which, more than any other, makes the lessons of the ROYAL ARCH MASON sublime.

The first of the difficulties of the return journey were the trials of the road itself. Upon other pages we have given, in our description of the journey to Babylon, sketches of the road rendered painful by sharp hills, arid deserts, and interminable distances. This is equally applicable here. Although the traveler had not the fitter accompaniments of chains, cruel guards, and hunger, yet no one can pass over the long way of eight hundred miles from Babylon to Jerusalem, even under favorable circumstances, without intense suffering. The introduction of the following Psalms at this stage of the drama is highly appropriate:

"Lord, I cry unto thee: make haste unto me; give ear unto my voice, when I cry unto thee. Let my prayer be set forth before thee as incense; and the lifting up of my hands as the evening sacrifice.

"Set a watch, O Lord, before my mouth; keep the

door of my lips. Incline not my heart to any evil thing, to practice wicked works with men that work iniquity: and let me not eat of their dainties.

"Let the righteous smite me; it shall be a kindness: and let him reprove me; it shall be an excellent oil, which shall not break my head: for yet my prayer also shall be in their calamities. When their judges are overthrown in stony places, they shall hear my words; for they are sweet.

"Our bones are scattered at the grave's mouth, as when one cutteth and cleaveth wood upon the earth. But mine eyes are unto thee, O God the Lord: in thee is my trust; leave not my soul destitute.

"Keep me from the snare which they have laid for me, and the gins of the workers of iniquity. Let the wicked fall into their own nets, whilst that I withal escape."—Psalm cxli.

"I cried unto the Lord with my voice; with my voice unto the Lord did I make my supplication. I poured out my complaint before him; I shewed before him my trouble.

"When my spirit was overwhelmed within me, then thou knewest my path. In the way wherein I walked have they privily laid a snare for me.

"I looked on my right hand, and beheld, but there was no man that would know me: refuge failed me; no man cared for my soul. I cried unto thee, O Lord: I said, Thou art my refuge and my portion in the land of the living.

"Attend unto my cry; for I am brought very low: deliver me from my persecutors; for they are stronger than I. Bring my soul out of prison, that I may praise thy name: the righteous shall compass me about; for thou shalt deal bountifully with me."—Psalm cxlii.

"Hear my prayer, O Lord; give ear to my supplications; in thy faithfulness answer me, and in thy righteousness. And enter not into judgment with thy servant; for in thy sight shall no man living be justified.

"For the enemy hath persecuted my soul; he hath smitten my life down to the ground; he hath made me to dwell in darkness, as those that have been long dead. Therefore is my spirit overwhelmed within me; my heart within me is desolate.

"I remember the days of old; I meditate on all thy works; I muse on the work of thy hands. I stretch forth my hands unto thee; my soul thirsteth after thee as a thirsty land. Selah.

"Hear me speedily, O Lord: my spirit faileth; hide not thy face from me, lest I be like unto them that go down into the pit. Cause me to hear thy loving-kindness in the morning, for in thee do I trust; cause me to know the way wherein I should walk, for I lift up my soul unto thee. Deliver me, O Lord, from mine enemies: I flee unto thee to hide me.

"Teach me to obey thy will; for thou art my God: thy Spirit is good; lead me into the land of uprightness.

"Quicken me, O Lord, for thy name's sake; for thy righteousness' sake bring my soul out of trouble. And of thy mercy cut off mine enemies, and destroy all them that afflict my soul: for I am thy servant."—Psalm cxliii.

The traverse of the long and weary wilderness and

the mountain-passes being accomplished, trials of a moral and religious character are suggested in the drama of the ROYAL ARCH. So many of the Jews had intermarried with their conquerors that great numbers of the people had lost the distinctive characteristic of the nation—a pure genealogy—and were necessarily rejected when they should offer themselves for a work that admitted none but the pure and undefiled. Before leaving Babylon, careful examinations had been made of the genealogical claims of every family, and those whose record was unquestioned were furnished with tests, by means of which they should have recognition of the High-Priest at Jerusalem. Of these the Royal Arch traditions are full. What the nature of those tests was can not, of course, be explained here.

Arrived at Jerusalem, where a tabernacle had been temporarily pitched among the Temple-ruins upon the Holy Hill, every person offering himself for the work was subjected to necessary examinations preparatory to his enrollment among the faithful.

Recurrence is now had to the history of Moses in his work of convincing the Egyptians and the Hebrews of his Divinely-appointed mission. Jehovah condescended to bestow upon him evidences of his power; Moses' rod was transformed to a serpent. When we enter into the world and discover around us the effects of the artifice of the tempter in the garden, and when we behold this arch-apostate transformed into a serpent, we have passed the first veil of our existence. The serpent referred to above was perpetuated as a Jewish symbol by Moses, who, in a terrible irruption of those venomous creatures into his camp, made a Brazen Serpent and set it upon a pole, that it might be seen from all parts of the camp, and then whoever was bitten was healed by simply *looking at the brazen figure.*

A second miracle was employed by Jehovah to strengthen the faith of Moses. He was directed to put his hand into his bosom, and when he took it out it was leprous as snow. On being commanded to put it the second time into his bosom and withdraw it, it was turned again as his other flesh. At the close of life, when we are called from this probationary scene and prostrated in the pallid leprosy of death, the second veil is drawn behind us. The leprosy is a loathsome and infectious disease, still prevalent in Oriental countries, corresponding in its general characteristics with the leprosy of former ages. The bones and the marrow are so pervaded with the virus of the disease that the joints of the hands and feet lose their power, the limbs of the body fall together, and the whole system assumes a most deformed and shocking appearance. There is at this day a small village of lepers, numbering in all about two hundred, on the outside of the southern wall of Jerusalem, near the Sion Gate. Their homes are miserable huts, low, dark, and loathsome. Allowed to marry only with each other, their offspring retain their health until arrived at the period of puberty, when the fatal disease makes its appearance, spreads over the system, ultimately reaches some vital organ, and the unhappy victim dies.

Among the miracles by which Moses convinced Pharaoh of the Divine appointment of his mission, that of taking water from the river Nile, and turning it into blood by pouring it upon the dry land, was one of the most stupendous. In the morning of the Resurrection, when the slumbering ashes shall revive, and we learn that the words of the woman of Tekoa are untrue, wherein she said "we are as water spilt upon the ground, which can not be gathered up," then shall the third veil be parted from us. The effect of this miracle was tremendous; the great river of Egypt was turned to blood.

The leader and governor of the first grand colony from Babylon was Prince Zerubbabel. In his name all the proceedings were had; the care of the sacred vessels intrusted to the Jews by King Cyrus, the money, provisions, etc., rested upon him. It follows that none could be accepted at Jerusalem save those who had come up under his patronage. The righteous in the last day will have the stamp of the signet of Heaven upon their foreheads, and be received by the Captain of their salvation. The prophet Haggai gives clear evidence of the Divine acceptance in which Zerubbabel was held when he says, "In that day will I take thee, O Zerubbabel, my servant, the son of Shealtiel, saith the Lord, and will take thee as a signet; for I have chosen thee." A signet was usually a ring, with some inscription upon it, used as a seal, by the delivery or transfer of which the highest offices in the kingdom were bestowed. The word is used figuratively in the Bible to denote an act, or token, or process of confirmation.

We have already alluded to the circumstance which had impaired the legitimacy of so many of the Jewish people. When Esther was made Queen by the King of Persia, though exalted to great honor, yet her line was thus rendered illegitimate according to the Jewish theory; her children could not inherit with their fathers. The lineage of every family, or list of ancestors, was preserved by the Jews with extraordinary care—not only because it was through Abraham that the privileges of the Jewish Church were transmitted, but chiefly because of the deep interest which was felt in the predictions concerning the Messiah, and the tribe or family from which he should spring. When, therefore, any presented themselves at the tabernacle among the ruins who could not distinctly trace up their descent, they were scornfully rejected. We have evidences of this in the contempt with which the services of the Samaritans were refused by Zerubbabel, who said: "Ye have nothing to do with us to build our house *unto our God;*" and in the case of a number of the children of priests "who sought their register among those that were reckoned by genealogy, but they were not found; therefore were they, as polluted, put from the priesthood."—Ezra, ii.

These sharp tests to which God's people were put, secured workmen of fidelity and zeal. No part of the labor, however arduous, servile, or protracted, was distasteful to them, and they entered upon the work with a determination that could have but one result—perfect success.

THE HIGH-PRIEST, KING, AND SCRIBE.

THE HIGH-PRIEST.—The three principal officers of the ROYAL ARCH CHAPTER, as the system is practiced in the United States, are known as the High-Priest, King, and Scribe. Upon the return of the captives from Babylon, Jeshua was High-Priest, a man full of fervency and zeal, who took a leading part at Jerusalem in rebuilding the altar of the Lord, and offering burnt-offerings thereon, as it is written in the law of Moses, the man of God. It is further recorded of this devoted servant of the Most High, that "In the second year of their coming into the house of God at Jerusalem, in the second month, began . . . Jeshua the son of Jozadak, . . . and appointed the Levites from twenty years old and upward to set forward the work of the house of the Lord."

"Then stood Jeshua with his sons . . . to set forward the workmen in the house of God."—Ezra, iii.

A further instance of the enlightened zeal of Jeshua is seen in his refusing the application of the Samaritans and others who proffered to build the Temple with them. The High-Priest, knowing their illegitimacy, sternly replied: "Ye have nothing to do with us to build a house unto our God; but we ourselves together will build unto the Lord God of Israel, as Cyrus the king of Persia hath commanded us."—Ezra, iv.

THE KING.—The King in a ROYAL ARCH CHAPTER represents Zerubbabel, one of the most distinguished characters described in Scripture. So prominent a part did he take during the period under consideration, in leading the first colony of Jews that returned from the captivity of Babylon, in preserving the sacred vessels intrusted by Cyrus to his charge, in laying the foundation-stone and cape-stone of the Temple, and in restoring the ancient religious rites of the nation, that the second Temple is familiarly styled *Zerubbabel's*, as the first is called *Solomon's Temple.* In the prophesy of Zechariah he is made the special subject of a Divine message. "This is the word of the Lord unto Zerubbabel, saying, Not by might or power, but by my spirit. Who art thou, O great mountain? before Zerubbabel thou shalt become a plain: and he shall bring forth the headstone thereof with shoutings, crying, Grace, grace unto it. Moreover, the word of the Lord came unto me, saying, The hands of Zerubbabel have laid the foundation of this house; his hands shall also finish it; and thou shalt know that the Lord of hosts hath sent me unto you. For who hath despised the day of small things? for they shall rejoice and shall see the plummet in the hand of Zerubbabel."—Zechariah, iv.

An affecting evidence of the Divine approval of this man is found in various passages in Haggai, a prophet sent with cheering tidings to Jeshua and Zerubbabel at a time when the people had begun to show signs of discouragement. Concerning the latter, Haggai said: "I will take thee, O Zerubbabel, my servant, saith the Lord, and will make thee as a signet; for I have chosen thee, saith the Lord of hosts."

THE SCRIBE.—The Scribe in a ROYAL ARCH CHAPTER, according to the American system, represents the prophet Haggai, to whom allusions have been made above. This celebrated personage is supposed to have been born during the captivity, and to have returned with Zerubbabel from Babylon. His prophesy ranks as the thirty-seventh in the order of the books of the Old Testament. It is principally composed of keen reproof and affecting exhortations respecting the building of the second temple, which the people had abandoned for fourteen or fifteen years, because of the opposition and intrigue of their enemies; and it also contains predictions of Christ and the universal establishment of his kingdom.

It is supposed that the glory of the temple, which is predicted by Haggai with great clearness, was to be occasioned by the coming of Christ; though Herod made important alterations in it, still the temple of Zerubbabel was always regarded as the second temple, and Christ, the Desire of all nations, did appear and teach in it.

The Book of Haggai well deserves to be read—it is very brief—at every meeting of a ROYAL ARCH CHAPTER. As a specimen of the symbolical style and nervous language with which the man of God urged forward his companions to their duty of rebuilding the temple and city, see the following:

"In the four and twentieth day of the ninth month, in the second year of Darius, came the word of the Lord by Haggai the prophet, saying: Thus saith the Lord of hosts, Ask now the priests concerning the law, saying, If one bear holy flesh in the skirt of his garment, and with his skirt do touch bread, or pottage, or wine, or oil, or any meat, shall it be holy? And the priests answered and said, No. Then said Haggai, If one that is unclean by a dead body touch any of these, shall it be unclean? And the priests answered and said, It shall be unclean. Then answered Haggai, and said, So is this people, and so is this nation before me, saith the Lord; and so is every work of their hands; and that which they offer there is unclean. And now, I pray you, consider from this day and upward, from before a stone was laid upon a stone in the temple of the Lord: since those days were, when one came to a heap of twenty measures, there were but ten; when one came to the press-fat for to draw out fifty vessels out of the press, there were but twenty. I smote you with blasting and with mildew and with hail in all the labors of your hands; yet ye turned not to me, saith the Lord. Consider now from this day and upward, from the four and twentieth day of the ninth month, even from the day that the foundation of the Lord's temple was laid, consider it. Is the seed yet in the barn? yea, as yet the vine, and the fig-tree, and the pomegranate, and the olive-tree, hath not brought forth: from this day will I bless you."—Haggai, ii.

Official Duties.—The official duties of these three prominent officers of the Royal Arch Chapter respectively are made as nearly as possible in analogy with those of the Jewish dispensation. The High-Priest is solemnly inducted with the following prayer:

"Most Holy and glorious Lord God, the Great High-Priest of heaven and earth, we approach thee with reverence, and implore thy blessings on the Companion appointed to preside over this assembly, and now prostrate before thee. Fill his heart with fear, that his tongue and actions may pronounce thy glory. Make him steadfast in thy service. Grant him firmness of mind; animate his heart and strengthen his endeavors. May he teach thy judgments and thy laws; and may the incense he shall put before thee, upon thine altar, prove an acceptable sacrifice unto thee. Bless him, O Lord, and bless the work of his hands. Accept us in mercy. Hear thou, from heaven, thy dwelling-place, and forgive our transgressions. Glory be to God the Father, as it was in the beginning, is now, and ever shall be, world without end. *Amen.*"

The High-Priest is then invested with the miter, breast-plate, and robe: the former reminding him of the dignity of his office and its inscription, "Holiness to the Lord"—of his dependence upon God; the breast-plate teaching him his responsibility to the laws of Royal Arch Masonry, and that its honor should ever be near his heart; the robes teaching him, by their symbolical colors, every grace and virtue that can beautify the human mind.

The King is taught by his scarlet robe, an emblem of imperial dignity, that paternal concern which he should feel for the welfare of his Chapter, and the ardent zeal with which he should endeavor to promote its prosperity; and by his crown, that to reign sovereign in the hearts and affections of men is made grateful to a generous mind, than to rule over their lives and fortunes, and that to do this with honor and satisfaction he must subject his own passions and prejudices to the dominion of reason and charity.

The Scribe is taught by his purple robe, an emblem of union, that the harmony and unanimity of the Chapter must be his care, and that he must endeavor to establish a permanent union among all degrees and orders in Masonry.

In the conclusion of the respective charges, a general address is delivered to the officers, as follows:

"Precept and example should ever advance with equal

pace. Those moral duties which you are required to teach unto others you should never neglect to practice yourselves. Do you desire that the demeanor of your equals and inferiors toward you should be marked with deference and respect? Be sure, then, that you omit no opportunity of furnishing them with examples in your own conduct toward your superiors. Do you desire to obtain instruction from those who are more wise or better informed than yourselves? Be sure, then, that you are always ready to impart of your knowledge to those within your sphere who stand in need of and are entitled to receive it. Do you desire distinction among your Companions? Be sure, then, that your claims to preferment are founded upon superior attainments. Let no ambitious passion be suffered to induce you to envy or supplant a companion who may be considered as better qualified for promotion than yourselves; but rather let a laudable emulation induce you to strive to excel each other in improvement and discipline, ever remembering that he who faithfully performs his duty, even in a subordinate or private station, is as justly entitled to esteem and respect as he who is invested with supreme authority."

In further allusion to these characters, the Scriptural accounts of the office of High-Priest established him as the head of the Jewish priesthood. All the male descendants of Aaron were by divine appointment consecrated to the priesthood; and the first-born of the family, in regular succession, was consecrated in the same manner to the office of High-Priest. The office was originally held for life, but this, as well as the right of the first-born, were disregarded in the latter ages of the Jewish nation. The High-Priest's most solemn, peculiar, and exclusive duty was to officiate in the Most Holy Place on the great day of atonement. He might at any time perform the duties assigned to the ordinary priests, but this one could be performed by himself alone. The High-Priest is supposed to have had an assistant to occupy his place in case of his incompetency from sickness, defilement, or otherwise.

The title King is that of a ruler. It is often applied in Scripture to the chief of a tribe, or the ruler of a single town or city. The title is preëminently applied to Jehovah and to our blessed Savior.

The term Scribe is first given to the king's secretary or messenger, and to such as excelled in the use of the pen; but, in time, it came to mean simply a learned man. It was the peculiar office of the priests and Levites not only to study the book of the law with great diligence, and to read and explain it to the congregation, but to transcribe it and to multiply copies among the nation at large. The scribes and the doctors of the law are terms often applied to the same class of people.

THE SPIRIT OF THE WORK.

The spirit of freedom, fervency, and zeal with which the labors of the ROYAL ARCH CHAPTER are supposed to be conducted, is conveyed in the following extracts from Paul's stirring exhortation to the Church at Thessalonica. This passage is statedly used in every Chapter of ROYAL ARCH MASONS:

"Now we command you, brethren, in the name of our Lord Jesus Christ, that ye withdraw yourselves from every brother that walketh disorderly, and not after the tradition which he received from us. For yourselves know how ye ought to follow us: for we behaved not ourselves disorderly among you; neither did we eat any man's bread for naught; but wrought with labor and travail night and day, that we might not be chargeable to any of you: not because we have not power, but to make ourselves an example unto you to follow us.

"For even when we were with you, this we commanded you, that if any would not work, neither should he eat.

"For we hear that there are some which walk among you disorderly, working not at all, but are busy-bodies.

"Now them that are such we command and exhort by our Lord Jesus Christ, that with quietness they work, and eat their own bread.

"But ye, brethren, be not weary in well-doing.

"And if any man obey not our word by this epistle, note that man, and have no company with him, that he may be ashamed.

"Yet count him not as an enemy, but admonish him as a brother.

"Now the Lord of peace himself give you peace always by all means. The Lord be with you all.

"The salutation of Paul with mine own hand, which is the token in every epistle: so I write.

"The grace of our Lord Jesus Christ be with you all. Amen."—2 Thessalonians, iii.

These exhortations convey the whole theory of the

ROYAL ARCH. The Veils of the Sanctuary, which make so prominent a display in the Chapter, suggest the most expansive benevolence, the most endearing union, the most transcendent zeal, the most spotless purity. The high value given to the Law ever open upon the Altar, the sight of the Ark, with its impressed traditions, the Pauline exhortations so charged with the very spirit of Divine love—all these combine to make the dramatic exercises healthful to the soul and conscience.

The following lines are among the older odes appropriated to this grade:

Joy, the Sacred Law is found:
  Now the Temple stands complete;
Gladly let us gather round
  Where the Pontiff holds his seat.

Now he spreads the volume wide,
  Opening forth the leaves to-day;
And the Monarch by his side
  Gazes on the bright display.

Joy, the Secret Vault is found;
  Full the sunbeams fall within,
Pointing darkly under ground,
  To the treasure we would win.

They have brought it back to light,
  And again it cheers the earth;
All its leaves are purely bright,
  Thriving in their newest worth.

This shall be the sacred Mark
  Which shall guide us to the skies;
Bearing like a holy Ark
  All the hearts who love to rise.

This shall be the Corner-stone
  Which the builders threw away,
But was found the only one
  Fitted for the Arch's stay.

This shall be the Gavel true,
  At whose sound the crowd shall bend,
Giving to the Law its due;
  This shall be the faithful friend.

This the Token that shall bring
  Kindness to the rich and poor;
Hastening on, on angel's wing,
  To the lone and darksome door.

This shall crown the mighty Arch
  When the Temple springs on high,
And the Brethren bend their march
  Wafting Incense to the sky.

Then the solemn strain shall swell
  From the bosom and the tongue,
And the Master's glory tell
  In the harmony of song.

Here the exile, o'er the waste,
  Trudging homeward shall repose;
All his toil and danger past,
  Here his long sojournings close.

Entering through the Sacred Veils
  To the holy cell he bends;
Then, as sinking nature fails,
  Hope in glad fruition ends.

THE ROBES OF THE HIGH-PRIEST.

In our sketch of the official duties of the High-Priest, a brief allusion was made to the emblematical bearing of his robes: "They taught him, by these symbolical colors, every grace and virtue that can beautify the human mind." Much is said in Scripture relative to the splendid and costly costume of the High-Priest. It was much more magnificent than that of the inferior order of priests. A description of it is best given in the words of Scripture:

"And of the blue, and purple, and scarlet, they made clothes of service, to do service in the holy place, and made the holy garments for Aaron; as the Lord commanded Moses.

"And he made the ephod of gold, blue, purple, and scarlet, and fine-twined linen.

"And they did beat the gold into thin plates, and cut it into wires, to work it in the blue, and in the purple, and in the scarlet, and in the fine linen, with cunning work.

"They made shoulder-pieces for it, to couple it together: by the two edges was it coupled together.

"And the curious girdle of his ephod, that was upon it, was of the same, according to the work thereof, of gold, blue, and purple, and scarlet, and fine twined linen; as the Lord commanded Moses.

"And they wrought onyx-stones inclosed in ouches of gold, graven as signets are graven, with the names of the children of Israel.

"And he put them on the shoulders of the ephod, that they should be stones for a memorial to the children of Israel; as the Lord commanded Moses.

"And he made the breast-plate of cunning work, like the work of the ephod; of gold, blue, and purple, and scarlet, and fine twined linen.

"It was four-square; they made the breast-plate double: a span was the length thereof, and a span the breadth thereof, being doubled."—Exodus, xxxix.

In addition to this description, which is elaborated in the subsequent verses, we may add that the ephod consisted of two plates, the one covering the back, the other the breast, both being united upon the two shoulders. It is sometimes described as having been thrown over the shoulders and hanging down before, crossed upon the breast. Upon the place where it crossed the breast was the breast-plate. This was a piece of embroidered work about ten inches square, with a front and lining to answer as a pouch. It was adorned with precious stones, described below. The upper corners were fastened to the ephod, from which it was not to be loosed: the two lower corners to the girdle. The breast-plate was called the Memorial, because it reminded the priest of his representative character in relation to the Twelve Tribes, and it was called the Breast-plate of Judgment, probably because worn by him who was instrumentally the fountain of judgment and justice to the Jewish Church.

The miter, or head-dress, was formed of eight yards of fine linen in circular folds, and inscribed in front, upon a plate of pure gold, the words "Holiness to the Lord."

The terms "Urim and Thummim" are associated with the breast-plate; but whether they denoted some Divine manifestation made in or upon the breast-plate itself, or whether it was a visible appendage to the breast-plate, indicating its peculiar and sacred use in this respect, is not known. The words literally signify "Lights and Perfections." The utmost that can be satisfactorily known respecting the subject is, that it was a manner or thing through which a knowledge of the Divine will was sought and conveyed. The twelve stones in the breast-plate were a sardius, topaz, carbuncle, the first row; emerald, sapphire, diamond, second row; ligure, agate, amethyst, third row; beryl, onyx, jasper, fourth and lower row.

Viewing these grand and enlivening symbolisms, the enlightened Freemason can not but wish his lot had been cast in the days when Freemasons were operative as well as speculative, and when God spoke through the mysterious Urim and Thummim as a man speaketh to his neighbor, face to face. In that spirit the following lines are offered:

Give me the Faith my fathers had,
  When home-worn ties were cast,
In stern contempt, forever back,
  Like chaff upon the blast.
These prayers, lip-measured, leave me chill,
As icy fount sends icy rill;
No passion bidding nature start,
No fire struck out to warm the heart;
There's nothing left to make me glad,
Give me the Faith my fathers had.

A patriot now is bought and sold
  For price; but give to me
The hopes that traced the hearts of old—
  My fathers' Liberty.
What's fine-drawn speech and wordy war?
A candle-ray to freedom's star!

The hand to hilt, the sword abroad,
The flag to heaven, the heart to God,
These are the tokens I would see;
Give me my fathers' Liberty.

Give my fathers' walk below:
  No artful mind was theirs,
To compass kindred hearts about
  With treachery and snares;
No nets of artifice they spread
To lure the innocent to tread;
Life's blessings they so freely shared,
Life's fears they boldly met and dared;
A blameless life, a death sublime,
These were the things of olden time.

Give me the friendships that entwined
  The upright trunks of yore,
The tendrils that so sweetly vined
  In beauty and in power.
My heart is sad to think this earth,
With all its joy, with all its mirth,
Has lost the chain our fathers wove—
The chain of holy, holy love;
Has lost the path our fathers trod—
The path that led them up to God.

O, then, bring back the palmy days
  Of innocence and truth,
When honesty was in its prime,
  And selfishness in youth;
When man allowed to man his place,
When probity unbared its face,
When Justice poised an equal scale,
When faith sang through the dying wail;
Away, this age of care and crime—
Give me the days of olden time!

THE TEMPLES UPON MOUNT MORIAH.

All that can be known of the Temple of Zerubbabel is, that, in style of architecture, it was as nearly as possible a copy of that which had been destroyed by Nebuchadnezzar nearly ninety years before. This Temple, in general form, resembled the Tabernacle, elaborately described upon another page. It was a substitute for the Tabernacle, which was only adapted to a wayfaring people, and was the great center of the same system of ceremonial worship. It was built upon Mount Moriah. This was one summit of a range of hills, the general name of which was Mount Sion. Beginning on the north, the ridge bears the name of Bezetha, then Moriah, then Ophel, the latter running down to the junction of the ravine termed the Tyropœon with the valley of Jehoshaphat. Mount Moriah has an altitude of about four hundred feet above the valley on the east.

The idea of building a Temple was suggested to the mind of David by the contemplation of his own good fortune, the general state of prosperity to which his country had arrived, and his fraternal relations with the Phœnician King Hiram, whose dominions afforded suitable wood and his subjects suitable workmen for the edifice. It became to David an object of lively and unceasing interest; and although he was not permitted by the Almighty to take a single step in its erection, yet he collected during the latter years of his reign precious metals to the value of many billions of dollars, besides immense quantities of brass, iron, stone, lumber, etc., and secured skillful artificers for every branch of the work. He also furnished the design, plan, and location of the building, in all which he was Divinely instructed.

The superintendence of the building was committed to his wise son Solomon, who in the fourth year of his reign laid the foundation-stone and began the work. Of laborers, native and foreign, there were in all 183,600. 30,000 of these were Jews, who worked in rotation—10,000 a month. 153,600 of them were Phœnicians; viz., 70,000 bearers of burdens, 80,000 hewers in wood and stone, and 3,600 overseers. The parts were all prepared at a distance from the site of the building, and when they were brought together, the whole immense structure was erected without the sound of ax, hammer, or any tool of iron. At the end of seven and one-half years it stood complete in all its splendor, the glory of Jerusalem, and the most magnificent edifice in the world.

The Temple, like the Tabernacle, had its front toward the east. The porch or portico extended across the whole front, projecting fifteen feet from the main building, and rising to the height of one hundred and eighty feet. Upon the sides and rear of the main building was an additional building of three stories, each nearly eight feet high. This structure was about half the height of the Temple, and, though built against the walls, was not fastened into them. It was divided into apartments like chambers, which opened into the gallery that surrounded it. There was a flight of stairs on the south side which led into the second story, and another leading from the second into the third. The whole building and its environs were entered by two courts. The inner court, called the Court before the Temple, or the Court of the Priests, corresponded generally with the Court of the

Tabernacle, as did also the sacred apartments, furniture, and utensils.

The Temple of Solomon was destroyed by Nebuchadnezzar, four hundred and twenty-four years after its completion. A second edifice, in breadth and height twice the size of Solomon's, was erected by Zerubbabel, being completed seventy-three years after the destruction of the last. But this lacked five great essentials of the other; viz., the Ark, the Mercy-seat, the Sacred Fire, the Urim and Thummim, and the visible revelation of the Divine glory, termed the Sheekinah. It was never blessed, either, with the spirit of prophesy like the former. This Temple stood without alteration for nearly five hundred years, when it became much decayed, and Herod the Great undertook its restoration. So large were the alterations made that it was in effect almost a new structure. He began the work seventeen years before Christ, and in less than ten years completed the main edifice, so that it could be occupied. The whole work occupied forty-six years.

The dimensions and description of this Temple are recorded in history with considerable minuteness. The outer wall, inclosing the whole, was about one-eighth of a mile square, and stood nearly forty feet about the ground. This wall being built up from the valley beneath, was, in places, six hundred or even seven hundred feet in height. In these walls were seven massive and costly gates, each fifteen feet wide and thirty high; an additional one in the east, termed the Beautiful Gate, was seventy-five feet high, of the finest metal, highly polished, and richly adorned. Piazzas stood against the wall clear around the hill, supported on the back by the wall itself, in front by a double row of columns; on the south side the supports were three rows of columns. The porch on the east side was called Solomon's.

The larger part of the area within these walls was vacant ground, completely paved with marble, and called the Court of the Gentiles, because all classes of persons were at liberty to enter it; but beyond the wall which separated this from the next court none but Jews could pass, under penalty of death.

The second court was inclosed by a wall, and termed the Court of the Women, because this was the nearest approach to the Temple that women could make, save when they brought a sacrifice. Here was the treasury, and this was the place where some of our Savior's most impressive discourses were delivered.

The next court toward the Sanctuary was the Court of Israel. The outer half of this court, which was separated from the inner by a low railing, was entered by common Israelites to attend upon particular services of religion; but the inner half, next to the Sanctuary, was called the Court of the Priests, into which none save the tribe of Levi could enter, unless when he came to offer his sacrifice before the altar. Even our Savior, who was of the tribe of Judah, had no privileges here more than the most ordinary Israelite; and wherever it is recorded of him that he entered the Temple, must be understood as confined to the outer part of the Court of Israel. Within the Court of the Priests stood the Altar of Burnt-Offering and the Brazen Laver.

Next came the Sanctuary, the materials of which were beautiful and costly beyond description. It was ninety feet high, ninety feet long, and thirty feet wide, divided into two compartments, separated from each other by a curtain or veil. One of these was termed the Holy Place, which occupied sixty feet of the whole length, and in which were the altar of incense, the golden candlestick, and the table of shew-bread; the other was the Most Holy Place, which measured thirty feet each way. Around the Sanctuary, on all sides except in front, was a structure of three stories high, like that attached to the first Temple, as before described, and a vast Porch extended along the front. The Porch was one hundred and fifty feet long, thirty wide, and at its highest elevation nearly one hundred and eighty feet. The majestic entrance to this Porch was one hundred and thirty-five feet by thirty-seven; it had no door.

This Temple was razed to its foundations by the Romans A. D. 70–1, and the site of it was made like a planed field.

The present inclosure of Mount Moriah, measured on four sides, is, on the east, 1,523½ feet; south, 916; west, 1,600; north, 1,038. The surface of the hill has a general declination toward the south and east. The walls at their base are about nine feet thick, and average fifty feet in height; at the south-east corner, seventy-seven feet. The walls rise twelve to fifteen feet above the hill. In the east wall is a magnificent gate, fifty-five feet wide, long since closed; no other gate appears in the east or south walls. The west wall has eight gates, the north three. There are three principal edifices within the Temple area, all being used for purposes of religion by the Turks. One near the south-western corner is termed Mosque El-Aksa. It is two hundred and eighty feet long by one hundred and eighty-three broad, and at its highest rises to about seventy feet. A domed building in the south-east corner is termed Sidna Issa. A number of smaller edifices are along the southern wall.

In the center, and traditionally over the site once occupied by the Temples of Solomon, Zerubbabel, and Herod successively, is Kubbet es-Sakhrah, or the Mosque of Omar. This stands upon a marble-paved platform ten feet high, which is ascended through eight portals, of Saracenic style, some of which are truly elegant. The Mosque is one hundred and seventy feet in diameter, and the same in height. The lower story or main body of the building is a true octagon, sixty-seven feet on a side and forty-six feet high; the central and elevated portion is circular. There are four doors and four porches, each facing a cardinal point, the southern one affording the main entrance. Immediately beneath the center of the dome is a singular object, being a portion of the original rock, which every-where else was levelled off when the surface of the mountain was first prepared under the eye of Solomon. This venerable relic, for what purpose left can only be conjectured, is sixty feet long from north to south, and fifty-five broad. Rising five feet above the marble platform, described above, the body of this fragment is about fifteen feet high. In its south-east corner is an apartment, chiseled from the solid rock, fifteen feet square and eight feet high, with a roof five feet thick; below this there is reason to believe another such excavation exists, such, perhaps, as the traditions of ROYAL ARCH MASONRY suggest.

To this, then, have the ancient glories of Mount Moriah come! after alternations of nearly three thousand years, Jerusalem having been seventeen times destroyed and rebuilt, all the wealth, the talent, the free-will offerings, the religious fervor, and the Masonic traditions of a hundred generations are reduced to a few semi-heathen mosques, a false ritual of worship, a ruined city, and a desolate land. How long, O Lord, how long?

FURNITURE OF THE SANCTUARY.

A collection of Masonic implements, furniture, jewels, etc., is a synopsis, emblematically conveyed, of the whole purpose of the Masonic Institution. These things remind the officers of their power and jurisdiction, warning them not to abuse their position, limiting their jurisdiction, and prescribing their conduct. They afford to them, and equally to the membership, copious topics of advice. A brother of any grade may descant upon the excellence of the Holy Writings as a rule of life, for those writings teach us that, being born upon a level, we should act upon a square, circumscribe our desires within the compass of nature's gifts poured from the horn of Divine plenty. He may learn therefrom to walk uprightly, suffering neither the pressure of poverty nor the avarice of riches to tempt the heart, even for a moment, to swerve from the line of rectitude suspended before them from the center of heaven. The division of time into equal and regular portions is to him a sure rule for securing the greatest good from the opportunities that are daily afforded him. The subjection of his passions and desires is too clearly taught to be misunderstood, and from his entrance through the north-western portals of the Lodge to the hour when he is carried by a sorrowing brotherhood to his final resting-place, every thing around him in Lodge, Chapter, Council, and Commandery, is a constant admonition of death, and the necessity for an early preparation.

THE ARK.—In the grades of Most Excellent Master, ROYAL ARCH MASON, and others following, the Ark becomes a prominent emblem. The original of this was constructed by Moses while on the way from Egypt to Canaan. It was a small chest made for a specific purpose, by the express command of Jehovah. It was three feet and nine inches long, two feet and three inches wide, the same in height. It was made of shittim wood, which is the Masonic Acacia, playing so important a part in the drama of the Master Mason, and was covered with plates of gold. A border or crown of gold encircled it near the top, and it was surmounted by the mercy-seat, which was of solid gold, and answered the purpose of a cover or lid to the ark. It will be seen by this description, which is a literal transcript from Biblical accounts, how unlike the proper form is the Ark usually found in our ROYAL ARCH assemblies. On each end of the mercy-seat was placed a golden image, representing a cherub facing upward and bending down over the Ark. Two wings of gold were attached to the body of the Ark on each side, through which passed the staves or poles that were used in carrying it from place to place. These were made of the same wood with the Ark, and overlaid in the same manner.

In the Ark Moses placed a golden pot, containing three quarts of manna; Aaron's rod, which miraculously budded, blossomed, and yielded fruit at once; and the tables of the testimony, otherwise called the tables of the Ten Commandments. But we learn, from 1 Kings, viii, that when it was placed in the Sanctum Sanctorum of Soloman's Temple, "there was nothing in the Ark, save the two tables of stone."

On the mercy-seat, which surmounted the Ark, rested the awful and mysterious symbol of the Divine presence.

The Temple of Zerubbabel did not contain the Ark. Whether it was seized among the spoils when the city was sacked, or whether it was secreted and afterward destroyed, history does not inform us. The traditions of Freemasonry only partially supply this hiatus in Scripture account.

Some comment upon the original contents of the Ark may be expected. The Holy Writings have been alluded to in various parts of this work. As the term was understood by Moses, it comprised only the Ten Commandments. As successive additions were made by himself, by Samuel, by Ezra, and perhaps others, the Holy Writings increased in number to embrace thirty-nine different works under the Old Dispensation. The New Testament Scriptures, numbering twenty-seven works, makes the complete catalogue of sixty-six. The older portion was conveniently divided by Jewish authors into the Law, the Prophets, and the Psalms. In American Lodges and Chapters the connected series of Old and New Testament Scriptures are always used; but the opened pages are invariably in the Old Testament. An account of the loss of the Holy Writings during the later years of the Jewish monarchy, and of their recovery under the good king Josiah, is given in 2 Chronicles, xxxiv. The Pot of Manna is referred to in Exodus, xvi: "Moses said, This is the thing which the Lord commandeth, Fill an omer of it to be kept for your generations; that they may see the bread wherewith I have kept you in the wilderness when I brought you forth from the land of Egypt. And Moses said unto Aaron, Take a pot, and put an omer full of manna therein, and lay it up before the Lord, to be kept for your generations. As the Lord commanded Moses, so Aaron laid it up before the testimony, to be kept." This manna was a substance miraculously furnished to the children of Israel on their journey through the wilderness, and designed as a substitute for bread, the material for which they could not raise during their journeyings. It is called "the bread rained from heaven."

The most remarkable things about the manna of the Israelites were, that double the quantity was supplied on the sixth day of the week, so that no one need break the Sabbath by going out in search of it; that on the Sabbath no manna fell from heaven; and that what they kept from the sixth to the seventh day remained sweet, while that kept from any other became offensive. All three of these miracles were wrought to attest the sanctity of the Sabbath. It is described as a small, round thing, as small as the hoar-frost on the ground, like coriander-seed, white, and the taste of it like wafers made with honey. It was ground in mills or beaten in a mortar, then placed in pans, in the shape of cakes, and baked. In gathering this food, each person was permitted to take what was necessary for his own use, not exceeding an omer, or about three quarts, for each member the family. If more was collected, the surplus was distributed to those who had less.

For forty years this miraculous supply of food was furnished daily to between three and four millions of people. It ceased while they were encamped at Gilgal, immediately after they had celebrated the passover for the first time in the land of promise.

The emblem of Aaron's Rod is suggestive to a Freemason of the progress of nature from youth to manhood, and from manhood to trembling decrepitude. Soon do the buds of infancy bloom on the cheek of youth; soon are the blossoms of time succeeded by the fruits of eternity.

THE KEY.

The emblem of the Key may be improved to impress upon the mind of a Royal Arch Mason the importance of those secrets which have been transmitted through thirty centuries, amidst bitter persecutions, for the benefit of the Sons of Light. As we have thus received them, untarnished by the touch of profane curiosity, and unimpaired by the revolution of time and human events, so must we deliver them, in all their purity and perfection, to the brethren who shall come after us, confident that they will never be divulged to the unworthy. The Key is an emblem often referred to in Scripture.

THE THREE SQUARES.

Allusion has been made upon another page to the use of these emblems. The traditions of Freemasonry are uniform, that the greatest possible care was exercised at the building of the Temple of Solomon, that every block should be made of exact dimensions to fill a specified place in the wall. Nor was it left to the fidelity and vigilance of one man, or the skill and implement of one man, to decide upon this; three persons at least passed judgment upon every ashlar before it went into the hands of him who was to cement it within the wall. The emblematical application of this is too apparent to need explanation. In practice no person can be admitted a member of the Masonic Order in any grade until he has passed the trying square of every person present at the ballot-test; a single objection would be fatal to his admission.

THE WORKING TOOLS.

Since the fiat of Heaven has gone forth, In the sweat of thy face shalt thou eat bread, it becomes us cheerfully to submit, laboring industriously in our respective callings. Labor is honorable, and to none more so than those who properly comprehend the theory of this grade. The pickax, crowbar, and spade are emblems suggesting to our minds the source from which come our food, metallic wealth, fuel, and other necessaries of life. They remind us, too, that we are of the earth, earthy, and that our bodies, when the purpose is accomplished for which we were placed on earth, will return to dust.

THE FAITHFUL REMEMBRANCE.

WE'LL lay thee down where thou shalt sleep
All tenderly and brotherly,
And woman's eyes with ours shall weep
The precious drops of sympathy;
We'll spread above the cedar boughs,
Whose emerald hue and rich perfume
Shall make thee deem thy resting-place
A downy bed, and not a tomb.

That ——— breast which hath supplied
  Thy wants from earliest infancy,
Shall open fondly and supply
  Unbroken rest and sleep to thee;
Each spring the flower-roots shall send up
  Their painted emblems toward the sky,
To bid thee wait upon thy couch
  A little longer patiently.

We'll not forget thee, we who stay
  To work a little longer here;
Thy name, thy faith, thy love shall lie
  On memory's tablets bright and clear;
And when o'erwearied by the toil
  Of life our heavy limbs shall be,
We'll come, and one by one lie down
  Upon dear mother earth with thee.

There we will slumber by thy side;
  There, reunited 'neath the sod,
We'll wait, nor doubt in His good time
  To feel the raising hand of God;
To be translated from this earth,
  This land of sorrow and complaints,
To the Celestial Lodge above,
  Whose Master is the King of Saints!

THE ORDER OF HIGH-PRIESTHOOD.

Although no one is entitled to receive the Order of High-Priesthood save a Royal Arch Mason who has been regularly elected to preside over a Chapter of Royal Arch Masons, yet there is so much in relation to it that will interest the Masonic reader, that we append a synopsis of the theory, purposes, and instructions of the Degree. It bears the same relation to the

Capitular system of Masonry that the Degree of Past Master bears to the Symbolical.

The Degree is conferred in a Council of High-Priests, of which the officers are President, Vice-President, Chaplain, Treasurer, Secretary, Master of Ceremonies, Conductor, Herald, and Sentinel. There is nothing in the robes, jewels, or decorations distinct from those employed in a Royal Arch Chapter. Not less than three members must be present to participate in the ceremonies.

The drama has reference to circumstances which occurred in the life of the Patriarch Abraham. In an invasion of the country around the Dead Sea by four eastern kings, his nephew Lot had been taken prisoner. Upon being informed of this, Abraham gathered what force was at his command, pursued the marauders, overtook them at Hobah, north of Damascus, and rescued Lot out of their hands. Returning to his abode, near Hebron, he was saluted, as he passed by Jerusalem, with blessings and good cheer from the venerable Melchisedec, Priest of the Most High God, who abode there. It has ever been one of the hidden problems of Scripture history who this man was, a mystery still further obscured by the strange language of Paul, who, in Hebrews vii, describes him, in symbolical terms, as "without father, without mother, without descent, having neither beginning of days nor end of life." But the theory that Melchisedec was Shem, the oldest son of Noah, who is supposed to have been alive at this period, has able supporters, and is the most likely of all.

In acknowledgment of the priestly dignity and more than Oriental hospitality of Melchisedec, displayed toward him "at the valley of Shaveh, which is the king's dale," Abraham paid him tithes of all the property he had rescued from the marauders, and received from his hands this sublime benediction: "Blessed be Abram of the most high God, possessor of heaven and earth; and blessed be the most high God which hath delivered thine enemies into thy hand."

As this is the oldest formula of a priestly benediction extant, the circumstance is made the foundation of an impressive and instructive Degree, whose covenants are prepared with uncommon force, whose means of recognition are exceedingly practicable and brief, and which, by teaching respect to the name of the Most High, benevolence to suffering brethren, and the duty of curbing those passions which tend to evil, is worthy of more study than it has heretofore received. The accompanying prayer is worthy of the connection:

"O thou supreme High-Priest of heaven and earth, enlighten us, we beseech thee, with the knowledge of thy truth, and grant that the members of this convention, and all others who are teachers in Israel, may be endowed with wisdom to understand and to explain the mysteries of our Order. Be with us in all our assemblies; guide us in the paths of rectitude, and enable us to keep all thy statutes and commandments while life shall last, and finally bring us to the true knowledge of thy holy and mighty name."

The prayer at anointing the candidate is equally appropriate:

"O Thou, who doth bless the fruitage of the olive and the vine to man's use, and doth give him refreshment and joy for his labor, bless now in a spiritual sense, we entreat thee, this application of oil and wine, that they may represent the times of refreshment from on high which thou wilt bestow upon thy faithful laborers in the moral vineyard. Give to all thy workmen courage and strength. Increase their zeal. Awaken them to the value of thy promises, that when the toils of life are ended they may hear thy welcome plaudits, 'Well done, good and faithful servants; enter ye into the joy of your Lord.' Amen."

The benediction employed in this grade of High-Priesthood is the Aaronic blessing:

"The Lord bless thee and help thee; the Lord make his face to shine upon thee, and be gracious unto thee; the Lord lift up his countenance upon thee, and give thee peace."

THE MYSTIC WORD.

The following is the oldest effusion extant, prepared to accompany the conferring of the grade of Royal Arch according to the American system. The suggestions and allusions to the esoterical matters of the grade are sufficiently obvious to the informed companion:

When Orient wisdom beamed serene,
  And pillowed strength arose,
When beauty tinged the glowing scene,
  And faith her mansion chose,

Exulting hands the fabric viewed,
  Mysterious powers adored,
And high the triple union stood
  That gave the Mystic Word.

Pale envy withered at the sight,
  And frowning o'er the pile,
Called murder up from realms of light,
  To blast the glorious toil.
With ruffian outrage joined in woe,
  They form the league abhorred,
And wounded science felt the blow
  That crushed the Mystic Word.

Concealment from sequestered care
  On sable pinions flew,
And o'er the sacrilegious grave
  Her veil impervious threw;
The associate band in solemn state
  The awful loss deplored,
And wisdom mourned the ruthless fate
  That whelmed the Mystic Word.

At length through time's expanded sphere
  Fair science speeds her way;
And warmed by truth's refulgence clear,
  Reflects the kindred ray.
A second fabric's towering height
  Proclaims the sign restored,
From whose foundation brought to light
  Is drawn the Mystic Word.

To depths obscure the favored trine
  A dreary course engage
Till through the Arch the ray divine
  Illumes the sacred page:
From the wide wonders of this blaze
  Our ancient signs restored,
The Royal Arch alone displays
  The long-lost Mystic Word!

THE VAULTS UNDER THE TEMPLE.

It has ever been a tradition among Jewish writers, and woven into various Masonic Degrees, that the hill termed Moriah, upon which the Temple stood, is excavated in vaults for mysterious purposes. Travelers, from Bishop Arculf, who visited Jerusalem near the close of the sixth century, down to the present time, have given tales of the native residents embodying allusions to this fact, but no one has furnished the world with a distinct account until within a few years. Dr. James T. Barclay, an American missionary, first discovered the opening to an immense series of excavations, which he has described in his City of the Great King, published in 1858. These caves open near the Damascus Gate, in the northern wall of the city, the entrance being under the wall, which is ten feet thick. The outer apartment is more than one thousand feet in diameter, the rock being all quarried out by art, and used doubtless in the construction of the city, the walls, and the Temple. Many blocks are still lying upon the floor of the quarry, squared and prepared for the builders' hands; others are partly cut from the wall, as if the workmen were called away before their task was finished. This quarry being considerably higher in its lowest place than the ground upon which the Temple stood, explains a ready method for moving down by a gentle descent the heavy material used in that work. The work of quarrying was apparently effected by an instrument resembling a pick-ax, with a broad, chisel-shaped end, as the spaces between the blocks were not more than four inches wide, in which it would be impossible for a man to work with a chisel and mallet. After being cut away at each side and at the bottom, a lever was probably inserted, and the combined force of three or four men could easily pry the block away from the rock behind. The stone is extremely soft and friable, nearly white, and very easily worked, but, like the stone of Malta and Paris, it hardens upon exposure. The marks of the cutting-instrument are as plainly defined as if the workman had but just ceased from his labor. The extreme length of this quarry, as far as explored, from the city wall, is not less than a quarter of a mile.

Under the site of the Temple are excavations remaining as remarkable as the building itself. Perhaps every portion of the Sacred Hill is thus undermined, although up to the present period only a portion has been explored. In the south-west corner of the Hill there is a broad avenue under ground, two hundred and fifty-nine feet long, forty-two wide, and thirty high. At the end of this, a flight of nine steps leads downward to another hall, fifty feet long and forty wide, supported in the center by a pillar cut from a single stone, twenty-one feet high and six in diameter. It is probable that further galleries will be found connecting this cavern with others upon the hills westward. In the south-east corner is a series of caves, including a vault, supported by fifteen rows of columns, making an apartment three hundred and nineteen feet by two hundred and fifty. Immediately under the ancient Temple is a cave twenty feet by six, near which, at the depth of sixty or seventy feet, is a cistern capable of holding two million gallons of water! Concerning this immense reservoir, a writer says: "There is nothing remaining of all the works of

Solomon which so impressively reflects his wonderful intellect as this lake under the Temple."

It is only of late years that a thorough and systematic course of explorations above and beneath Jerusalem has been commenced. Fanaticism and barbarous exclusion are fast giving way before the light of civilization, and it can not be long until the Turkish rulers will submit to the various arguments of steel and gold urged upon them by throwing open the city to explorers. Then will be seen that the traditions of Freemasonry, which so long preserved important topographical, architectural, and religious knowledge concerning the ancient Hill, are well founded, and it is not beyond the bounds of credibility that discoveries await us as important in the advancement of Masonic Science as in general information.

THE THIRD ORDER IN FREEMASONRY.

THE CRYPTIC DEGREES:

CONSISTING OF

THE ROYAL MASTER

AND

THE SELECT MASTER.

THESE two Degrees are conferred, according to the American system, in a Council of Cryptic Masonry. The ballot is taken in the Second or Select Master's Degree; the same rules of balloting being observed as in the Symbolical Lodge.

All discipline exercised by a Lodge or Chapter requiring suspension and expulsion is indorsed by the Council without inquiry. The Council has also its own code of discipline for offenses against its laws.

Not less than nine nor more than twenty-seven members can open, work, or close a Council of Cryptic Masonry.

THE ROYAL MASTER.

WHAT AFTER DEATH?

WE can predict, from day to day,
Some things will meet us on life's way;
But who, of all that draw life's breath,
Can shadow *what is after death?*

When spring awakes we look for flowers,
And leafy boughs and genial bowers;
The flowery spring rewards our faith;
What shall we look for *after death?*

When autumn spreads its sober skies,
With open laps we wait the prize;
We catch the showering fruits beneath;
What fruitage for us *after death?*

We trace the infant through each stage
Of youth, of manhood, and of age;
Each stage confirms our previous faith—
What grade awaits him *after death?*

Such the reflections of this grade;
Such question here is freely made;
Life's SECRET lies beneath, beneath,
'T is only yielded *after death!*

THE ROYAL MASTER.

THE THEORY OF THE DEGREE OF ROYAL MASTER.

THE Degree of ROYAL MASTER is the beginning of a third series, of which the Symbolical Degrees and the Capitular or Chapitral Degrees are the first two. As a distinctive title, that of *Cryptic Degrees* has been generally adopted, as referring to the introduction of *caves* or *caverns* peculiar to this system. The Ritual is simple, but expressive. The introduction of the Cryptic Degrees into this country dates from a period about twenty years subsequent to that of the Royal Arch. The rule was then established that none but Royal Arch Masons should receive it. As a grade, it is preparatory to that of Select Master, bearing the same relation to it which the Degree of Entered Apprentice bears to that of Fellow Craft. Its means of recognition are used as a convenient and expeditious method of examining a Royal Arch Companion. The title of the organization in which the Degrees of Royal and Select Master are conferred, is *Council of Royal and Select Masters.* In a Council not more than nine nor less than twenty-seven members can take part at a time; if more be present, they are supernumerary. The government of Councils is intrusted to Grand Councils of Cryptic Masonry, of which there is one in nearly every State.

Mr. Cole informs us that in 1817 the Degree of ROYAL MASTER was "considered as merely preparatory, and usually conferred immediately before the solemn ceremony of exaltation to the Royal Arch." At that period it was conferred with the Degree of "Ark Master or Noachite," both being considered of equal authority. The latter has become obsolete in this country.

PRAYER.—The frequent repetition of prayer, in all the Masonic grades, is peculiarly calculated to impress the memory with our constant obligation to piety and devotion. Were the benefactions of Providence but partially or unfrequently enjoyed, perhaps we might forget that return of gratitude which is the only remuneration in our power to make; but his benefits are new every morning and fresh every moment, and surely our *perpetual* thanksgiving should ascend to heaven.

The voice of the Temple the tidings of love,
That speaks of the Master who reigneth above;
His glory, His glory in the highest who dwells,
And Good-will to man, is the burden it tells.
Come, Brethren, in chorus,
Prolong the glad tidings,
No duty so sweet as the hymning of God;
His faith each professing,
His knowledge possessing,
Exalt each the blessing His grace hath bestowed.

The meeting of a Lodge of ROYAL MASTERS is, in strictness, a religious ceremony. It can not be regularly opened or closed without prayer. The book of Holy Scriptures is an essential part of its furniture, without which no work can be done or instruction attempted. Blasphemy is deemed a heinous offense against the precepts of this grade. The Lodge of ROYAL MASTERS is, theoretically, a beacon-light, throwing abroad its rays, as from a mountain summit.

A city set upon a hill
  Can not be hid;
Exposed to every eye, it will
Over surrounding plain and vale
  An influence shed;
And spread the light of peace afar,
Or blight the land with horrid war.

This ROYAL LODGE is planted so,
  For high display;
It is a Beacon-light to show
Life's weary wanderers as they go
  The better way;
To show by ties of earthly love,
How perfect is the *Lodge above.*

Be this your labor, ROYAL FRIENDS,
  While laboring here;
Borrow from him who kindly lends
The heavenly ladder that ascends
  The higher sphere;
And let the world your progress see,
Upward by Faith, Hope, Charity!

RECOGNITIONS.—The members of this branch possess infallible means of recognition, equally applicable to the grades preceding. They are unchangeable, consistent with each other, and with a general plan, and they form a part of the instruction communicated to every ROYAL MASTER upon his reception into the Lodge. A visitor endeavoring to enter without a competent knowledge of these is viewed as an impostor, and contemptuously rejected; a visitor possessing them is hailed as a ROYAL MASTER, and welcomed accordingly.

Yet the outside world are not to suppose that the mere possession of a few private formulas of word and gesture are sufficient to entitle a person to conceive himself a brother. No. These are but the *sequalæ* of initiation. The whole system is far more elaborate, comprising a petition for initiation, avouchals, and recommendations, cautious inspection of moral character, and of physical and mental qualifications, the ballot thorough and secret, the reception traditional and impressive, and a series of covenants, than which nothing can be better devised to bind the conscience of a man to good thoughts and good works. These, accompanied with elaborate ritualisms, lead, in the end, to the communication of appropriate *means of recognition*, so arranged that while they suggest to the memory the peculiar secrets of the grade, are a constant reminder of its covenants and duties, and the punishment symbolically predicted of those who willfully violate and neglect them.

The means of recognition may be compared, in their unchangeableness and allegorical character, to the Pillars of King Solomon's Porch. The raising Pillars and Obelisks was a custom of the eastern nations, and of Egypt in particular; the use of which, we are told, was to record the extent of dominion and the tributes of nations subject to the Egyptian empire, etc., or in commemoration of memorable events. Diodorus tells us that Sesostris signalized his reign by the erection of two obelisks, which were cut with a design to acquaint posterity of the extent of his power, and the number of the nations he had conquered. Augustus, according to the report of Pliny, transported one of these obelisks to Rome, and placed it in the Campus Martius. Pliny says the Egyptians were the first devisers of such movements, and that Mestres, King of Heliopolis, erected the first. Marsham and others attribute the invention to Sesostris. The obelisk of Shannesis exceeded all that had preceded it; Constantine, and Constans, his son, caused it to be moved to Rome, where it remains, the noblest piece of Egyptian antiquity existing in the world. Solomon had pursued this custom in erecting his pillars in the porch of the Temple, which he designed should be a memorial to the Jews as they entered the Holy Place, to warn their minds with confidence and faith by this record of the promises made by the Lord unto his father David, and which were repeated unto him in a vision, in which the voice of God proclaimed, "I will establish the throne of thy kingdom upon Israel forever."

SCRIPTURAL REFERENCES.—The use of Scriptural passages in the Rituals of Masonry has a twofold application. It conveys to the initiate the peculiar instructions of the grade, often in the most forcible and direct manner, while it gives a clue to the memory in recalling the means of recognition. In this double sense the following passages are appropriate to the degree of ROYAL MASTER:

"And I heard a great voice out of heaven, saying, Behold, the tabernacle of God is with men, and he will dwell with them, and they shall be his people, and God himself shall be with them, and be their God.

"And God shall wipe away all tears from their eyes; and there shall be no more death, neither sorrow, nor crying, neither shall there be any more pain: for the former things are passed away.

"And he that sat upon the throne said, Behold I make all things new. And he said unto me, Write: for these words are true and faithful.

"And he said unto me, It is done. I am Alpha and Omega, the beginning and the end. I will give unto him that is athirst of the fountain of the water of life freely.

"And behold, I come quickly; and my reward is with me, to give every man according as his work shall be.

"I am Alpha and Omega, the beginning and the end, the first and the last.

"Blessed are they that do his commandments, that they may have right to the tree of life, and may enter in through the gates into the city."—Revela. xxi and xxii.

"And Solomon made all the vessels that pertained unto the house of the Lord: the altar of gold, and the table of gold, whereupon the shew-bread was, and the candlesticks of pure gold, five on the right side, and five on the left, before the oracle, with the flowers, and the lamps, and the tongs of gold; and the bowls, and the snuffers, and the basins, and the spoons, and the censers, of pure gold; and the hinges of gold both for the doors of the inner house, to-wit, of the temple. So Hiram made an end of doing all the work that he had made king Solomon for the house of the Lord."—1 Kings, vii.

"Lord, who shall abide in thy tabernacle? who shall dwell in thy holy hill?

"He that walketh uprightly, and worketh righteousness, and speaketh the truth in his heart.

"He that backbiteth not with his tongue, nor doeth evil to his neighbor, nor taketh up a reproach against his neighbor.

"In whose eyes a vile person is contemned: but he honoreth them that fear the Lord. He that sweareth to his own hurt, and changeth not.

"He that putteth not out his money to usury, nor taketh reward against the innocent. He that doeth these things shall never be moved."—Psalms, xv.

THE CHERUBIM.

THE consideration of the Cherubim as the most sacred emblem in the Mosaic Ceremonial is a part of the Rituals of the ROYAL MASTER. A group of Cherubims, in allusion to those that stood in the Holy of Holies, forms a proper emblem of this grade. The Cherub was a figure composed of various creatures, as a man, an ox, an eagle, or a lion. The first mention of the Cherubs is in Genesis, iii, 24, where the figure is not described; but their office was, with a flaming sword, to keep or guard the way of the tree of life. The two Cherubs which Moses was commanded to make, at the ends of the mercy-seat, were to be of beaten work of gold; and their wings were to extend over the mercy-seat, their faces toward each other, and between them was the residence of the Deity. (Exodus, xxv.) The Cherubs in Ezekiel's vision had each four heads or faces, the hands of a man and wings. The four faces were the face of a bull, that of a man, that of a lion, and that of an eagle. They had the likeness of a man. (Ezekiel, iv and ix.) In 2 Samuel, xxii, 11, and Psalm xviii, Jehovah is represented as riding on a Cherub and flying on the wings of the wind. In the celestial hierarchy Cherubs are represented as spirits next in order to Seraphs. The hieroglyphical and emblematical figures embroidered on the veils of the Tabernacle are called Cherubs of curious or skillful work. (Exodus, xxvi.)

The Scriptural accounts of the position of the Cherubims are precise:

> "He set the Cherubims within the inner-house; and they stretched forth the wings of the Cherubims, so that the wing of the one touched the one wall, and the wing of the other Cherub touched the other wall; and their wings touched one another in the midst of the house."—1 Kings, vi.

This should be an accurate guide to Royal Masters in the use of this emblem in their Lodges.

The Thought of Death.—There is no portion of the Ritual of Royal Master so impressive as the solemn thought of death, so aptly introduced. "The young *may* die, the old *must* die," is said with an impressiveness that is very affecting. To the most of men the end of life is anticipated with horror, insomuch that thousands of mankind would relinquish the opportunity of gaining an inheritance "incorruptible, undefiled, and that fadeth not away," if the present life could be immortal. Not so with the truly good man. He anticipates a season of rest and relief from mortal labors, when the grosser implements of sublunary arts shall be suspended in the desolated halls of mortality that the harps of angels may employ his hands forever. There, there will be no more occasion for level or plumb-line, for trowel or gavel, for compass or square. On the perfect level of eternity neither weakness nor envy will jeopardize the good man's bright career, nor will he need an emblem of rectitude while the example of sister-spirits is ever before him. The cement of heavenly love will be spread by the hand of Deity, and no imperfection will require the force of art to remove it. Infinitely broad will be the circle of duty, and no brother will be disposed to overleap its boundaries, for all will be kept within the angle of perfection by Him who is able "to keep us from falling" and present us faultless before the presence of His glory with exceeding joy. There the General Grand Lodge of immortality will hold an endless communication, consisting of the fraternity of the accepted of God.

By the pallid hue of those
Whose sweet blushes mocked the rose;
By the fixed, unmeaning eye,
Sparkled once so cheerfully;
By the cold damps on the brow,
By the tongue, discordant now;
By the gasp and laboring breath,
What, O tell us, what is death?

By the vacancy of heart,
Where the lost one had a part;
By the yearnings to retrieve
Treasures hidden in the grave;

By the future, hopeless all,
Wrapped as in a funeral pall;
By the links that rust beneath,
What, O tell us, what is death?

By the echoes swelled around,
Sigh and moan and sorrow-sound;
By the grave that, opened nigh,
Cruel, yields us no reply;
By the silent King, whose dart
Seeks and finds the mortal part;
We may know, no human breath
Can inform us what is death!

But the grave has spoken loud;
Once was raised the gloomy shroud,
When the stone was rolled away,
When the earth in frenzied play
Shook her pillars to awake
Him who suffered for our sake;
When the veil's deep fissure showed
All the mysteries of God!

Tell us, then, thou sink of hope,
What is He that breaks thee up?
Mortal, from my chambers dim
Christ arose, inquire of him!
Hark unto the earnest cry,
Notes celestial make reply:
Christian, unto thee 't is given—
Death 's a passage unto Heaven!

THE CUNNING WORKMAN.—In all the Masonic Degrees that relate to the building of the first Temple, particularly those of the Fellow Craft, the Master Mason, the Mark Master, the Royal Master, and the Select Master, there is much said in praise of the skill, assiduity, and fidelity of one known in the Scripture accounts as Hiram, the Widow's Son. The Biblical narrative concerning this remarkable man is as follows:

"And Solomon sent and fetched Hiram out of Tyre.

"He was a widow's son of the tribe of Naphtali, and his father was a man of Tyre, a worker in brass; and he was filled with wisdom, and understanding, and cunning to work all works in brass. And he came to Solomon, and wrought all his work."—1 Kings, vii.

"Now I have sent a cunning man, endued with understanding, of Huram my father's.

"The son of a woman of the daughters of Dan, and his father was a man of Tyre, skillful to work in gold, and in silver, in brass, in iron, in stone, and in timber, in purple, in blue, and in fine linen, and in crimson; also to grave any manner of graving, and to find out every device which shall be put to him, with thy cunning men, and with the cunning men of my lord David thy father." 2 Chronicles, ii.

This man, to the description of whose scientific knowledge and experienced art more space is given than to any other character in the Old Testament save Moses and Daniel, was intrusted with all the works in brass, the pillars Jachin and Boaz, the molten sea, the ten vases, the ten lavers, the pots, the shovels, and the basins of the Temple. In addition to these, it may safely be affirmed that the general superintendence of the entire erection was placed in his charge; the preparation of the veils, the engravings of all kinds, the settings of gems and precious stones, the construction of the ivory throne, the substructures of the Temple, the Cherubims, and, in brief, the whole work to which so much time, labor, genius, and expenditure were given. In this view, he was the most remarkable man, considered as a practical mechanic, or, as the Scriptures term it, "cunning workman," that the world ever produced. It is as natural to attribute to the Divine Providence the great qualities of the Builder Hiram as those of the Monarch Solomon; and it is difficult to see how such a work could have been constructed at all but for his superintendence.

The Scriptures and Church traditions are silent as to the ultimate history of the "cunning workman." Traditions connected with the apocryphal systems of "the Scotch Rite" describe him as returning to Phœnicia and constructing various temples after the completion of Solomon's, but the tradition of the Master Mason's Degree is positive that he did not outlive the completion of his *chef-d'œuvre* upon Mount Moriah. The circumstances of his death, as detailed in the Master's Lodge, are particularly interesting to the Royal Master, who is made acquainted with many amiable traits of his character, and exhorted to use him as a model of piety, industry, and fidelity to truth. In the capacity of a model, "the Widow's Son" is the most prominent figure in the Masonic Rituals. Every thing connected with his career while at Jerusalem—his wonderful assiduity to business, his frugality, his artistic skill, his accuracy in adapting means to ends, his modesty in his daily contact with kings, his unflinching attachment to discipline, without which so great a work must have miscarried, and, best of all, his fidelity to his trust as a speculative workman in a structure that was to survive the ruin of the Temple and the nation—all these are traits in the model character of Hiram. In many respects he is a prototype of the "Man of Galilee," whose Reign of Peace was prefigured by the period of King Solomon, and who, as Chief Architect of a religious structure that will defy eternity to shake it from its base, is the head of all speculative architecture; whose traditions are the history of the Church militant, and into whose glorious edifice we also, as "the fellow-citizens with the saints and of the household of God, are built upon the foundation of the apostles and prophets, Jesus Christ himself being the chief corner-stone, in whom all the building being fitly framed together, groweth unto a holy temple in the Lord." From these thoughts we naturally deduce the moral that Masonry was never intended to displace or supersede Christianity. It may, and often does, subserve the interests of the Cross, but can never fill its place or answer its ends. So far from setting up any such pretensions, it distinctly and unequivocally avows the contrary; and he who trusts to the moral power of Freemasonry for the revolution of his moral nature, the subjugation of his evil passions, and for a blissful immortality, poorly understands the ground-work of the Order, and works a fatal, unpardonable fraud upon himself.

THE SELECT MASTER.

AT MIDNIGHT AS AT NOON.

At midnight as at noon
  The ancient worthies met:
The glances of the moon
  Beheld those laborers late;
Nor till the glancing moon was high
Did any lay his Trowel by.

Each felt a weight of care,
  A solemn charge o'erspread;
Each toiled in earnest there,
  With busy hand and head;
And to the deep and faithful cave
These midnight craft a secret gave.

In whom the fire burns bright,
  At midnight as at noon,
All secrets come to light
  Beneath the glancing moon:
Nor till the glancing moon is high,
Must any lay his Trowel by.

THE SELECT MASTER.

THEORETICAL SKETCH OF NINE DEGREES.

THE system of accumulated Degrees is so popular in the United States, that it is rare to find a Master Mason who has not taken the "Higher Degrees," or who is not preparing to do so. This shows that it is not for practical purposes alone that our countrymen pursue Freemasonry—for all that is practical in the system is contained in the first three Grades—but for dramatic enjoyment and for those eclectic purposes which are subserved by the "Higher Degrees." This fact demands that we should, upon this last page, give a synopsis of the entire system of Nine Degrees usually accepted as a series of Grades in American Masonry.

1. THE ENTERED APPRENTICE.—This is the foundation-stone of the whole system; it is the trial Degree. Not less than seven must be associated together in a Lodge to confer it. The theory of it is *trial and moral discipline.* The working tools or practical symbols are the Twenty-four-inch Gauge and the Gavel. The instructions are Faith, Hope, and Charity; Brotherly

Love, Relief, and Truth; Temperance, Fortitude, Prudence, and Justice.

2. The Fellow Craft.—This is the complement of the preceding Degree; it is the Apprentice turned Journeyman. Not less than five must be associated together in a Lodge to confer it. The theory of it is *ability to shape perfect work.* The working tools or practical symbols are the Plumb, Square, and Level. The instructions are the Attentive Ear, the Instructive Tongue, and the Faithful Breast.

3. The Master Mason.—This is the governing Grade of the two preceding; it is the Fellow Craft placed in command of his fellows. Not less than three must be associated together in a Lodge to confer it. The theory of it is *ability to govern in the love and fear of God.* The working tool or practical symbol is the Trowel. The instructions are Friendship, Morality, and Brotherly Love.

4. The Mark Master.—This is the complement, in ritualism, of the Fellow Craft; it is the Fellow Craft made skillful. Not less than eight must be associated together in a Lodge to confer it. The theory of it is *good labor merits good wages.* The working tools or practical symbols are the Chisel and Mallet.

5. The Past Master.—This is the governing Grade of the four preceding; it is the Master Mason fitted to command a Lodge or many Lodges. Not less than three must be associated together in a Lodge to confer it.

The theory of it is that *a Masonic governor has three guides to discipline; viz., the Law of God, the Grand Lodge Constitution, and the By-Laws of his own Lodge.*

6. The Most Excellent Master.—This is closely connected with the Master Mason's Grade. Not less than two must be associated together in a Lodge to confer it. The theory of it is *fervent devotion to God.* The working or practical symbol is the Pot of Incense.

7. The Royal Arch Mason.—This is a continuation of the Master Mason; it is the Master Mason placed under circumstances of exile, hard pilgrimage, persecution, and excessive labor. Not less than nine must associate together in a Chapter to confer it. The theory of it is *unbounded devotion to God.* The working tools, or practical symbols are the Pickax, Spade, and Crowbar. The instructions are Freedom, Fervency, and Zeal.

8. The Royal Master.—This is a recurrence to the Grade of Fellow Craft; it is the Fellow Craft urgent for more light. Not less than nine nor more than twenty-seven must associate together in a Council to confer it. The theory of it is *ardent cravings for Masonic instruction.*

9. The Select Master.—This is the complement of the Grade of Royal Master; it is the Royal Master satisfied with light. Not less than nine nor more than twenty-seven must associate together in a Council to confer it. The theory of it is Justice and Mercy at ac-

cord. The working tools or practical emblems, both for this and the preceding grade, are the Trowel within the Triangle.

To sum up the theories, or central rays, of these nine grades, they are:

1. Trial and moral discipline.
2. Ability to shape perfect work.
3. Ability to govern in the love and fear of God.
4. Good labor merits good wages.
5. The three fundamental guides to discipline.
6. Fervent devotion to God.
7. Unbounded devotion to God.
8. Ardent cravings for Masonic instruction.
9. Justice and mercy at accord.

These are all good lessons, whose contemplation can not fail to improve the mind, soften the heart, restrain prejudices, increase the virtues, and fit the soul for higher labors in the Lodge above. In each Degree, the necessity and duty of prayer are impressed upon the mind of the novitiate, being as clearly important to the aged as to the young, on the borders of the grave as in the flower of manhood. It was pointed out to man, in the earliest ages of the world, as a suitable medium of communion between earth and heaven. It was the "Ladder of the Patriarch," on which angels descend to minister to the happiness of men. Its three rounds are adapted to the flight of the soul to its immortal mansions. Its benefits are immeasurable, and its obligatory force is commensurate with probationary being. It can never be useless or unimportant, till we have passed through the veils to repose on the bosom of our Maker.

COVENANTS.—There is also to each grade a series of Covenants, of which, in the cautious spirit of American Masonry, we can say but little. They are derived from Holy Writ, strongly enjoined upon the novitiate, and repeated with variations of language and sentiment in each Degree. They are such as none but a conscientious man, walking and working in the fear of God, can keep.

RECOGNITIONS.—In these grades there is also a series of methods of recognition, arrangements of tests, words, gestures, etc., by which the brethren of the respective Degrees may mutually examine and be examined for all the purposes of the society, without liability to error. Of these, no more can be said in print.

QUALIFICATIONS.—A general summary of the qualifications requisite to admission into any of these nine grades is thus given: It is formed out of the antiquated documents of Freemasonry extant, especially the "Ancient Charges," a publication, the oldest in Masonic science, made by authority of the Grand Lodge of England, in 1723. An applicant for the honors and privileges, the duties and responsibilities of Masonry, must be:

1. *A Man.* "No woman."

2. *Free, and Free-born.* "No bondman." "The owner of a bondman might otherwise seize him, even in the Lodge." "Free-born." "No bondsman."

3. *Of suitable age.* "Of mature and discreet age."

4. *Of good moral character.* "Good and true men." "No immoral or scandalous men." "No thief, robber,

or murderer." "Utter no false oaths." "Must reverence God." "Must work honestly." "Do no evil." "Not commit whoredom." "No thief nor the aid of a thief." "True men to God and the Church." "Know no treason or treachery." "No common player at the cards, dice, hazard, or any other unlawful plays."

5. *Born in honest wedlock.* "No bastard." "Descended of honest parents." "Of a good kindred." "Of honest parentage."

6. *Of good public estimation.* "Of good report." "No man under evil report." "Ignorance would discredit the Craft." "Honor is to be done to the Fraternity by itinerant Masons." "False oaths would bring disgrace upon Masonry." "No persons shall be accepted a Freemason but such as are of good reputation."

7. *Perfect in body.* "A perfect youth, having no maim or defect in his body." "On no account receive a mutilated person." "His limbs must be quite entire and shapely; it would be a stigma upon the Fraternity to initiate a halt or lame man." "Of limbs whole, as a man ought to be." "Able in all degrees, having his right limbs, as a man ought to have." "Of able body."

8. *Of good mental powers.* "If the Master discover that he is a Craftsman not so perfect as he should be, let him be at once discharged." "The Apprentice must be thoroughly instructed in the various points of the Masonic science." "He must keep the secrets intrusted to him."

9. *Submissive to Masonic rule.* "Willing to serve seven years." "An Apprentice must serve for smaller wages than a Fellow Craft." "He must exercise meek-

ness." "He must avoid discord and contention." "He must be constrained to appear wheresoever he is summoned." "If he in any wise contend against the ordinances of the Grand Lodge, he shall be made a subject of Masonic punishment." "He shall conceal and hide."

From this summary, the entire code of Masonic discipline and duty may be deduced. Nothing more perfect has ever been presented by human hands for human adoption, and so long as the labors of the Craft are performed upon this model, the Masonic Institution will stand a monument, from age to age, of social ties, mutual benefit, and moral perfection.

THE THEORY OF THE DEGREE OF SELECT MASTER.

The Degree of SELECT MASTER is the ninth and last of the series contemplated in the present volume. Beyond it, there is one Degree in the Chivalric System, termed the *Red-Cross Knight*, which bears the same relation to the Royal Arch that the Royal Master's Degree bears to the SELECT MASTER. But our present plan excludes it from this volume.

The Degree of SELECT MASTER, in beauty and impressiveness, does not lose in comparison with any other named in the present volume. Its *drama* is peculiarly interesting, suggesting to the mind the greatest doctrine of the Holy Scriptures; viz., the blending of mercy with justice. Mr. Webb's discription of it is as follows: "This Degree is the summit and perfection of ancient Masonry; and without which, the history of the Royal

Arch can not be complete. It rationally accounts for the concealment and preservation of those essentials of the Craft which were brought to light at the erection of the second Temple, and which lay concealed from the Masonic eye four hundred and seventy years. Many particulars relative to those few who, for their superior skill, were selected to complete an important part of King Solomon's Temple are explained. And here, too, is exemplified an instance of justice and mercy by our ancient Patron toward one of the Craft, who was led to disobey his commands by an over-zealous attachment for the institution. It ends with a description of a particular circumstance which characterizes the Degree." Mr. Cole describes the Degree of SELECT MASTER as "filling up a chasm which every intelligent Royal Arch Mason has observed. Without it, it seems difficult, if not impossible, to comprehend clearly some of the mysteries that belong to the august Degree of Royal Arch." He adds: "Such is the nature of this Degree, that we can not feel freedom to allude remotely to the nature of its secrets; we may, however, pronounce it the Key to the Arch." In 1817 it was conferred only in the city of Baltimore, Maryland, where it ranked as the Fifth Degree in the series, following next to that of Mark Master. In a subsequent page, Mr. Cole says: "Without the Degree of SELECT MASTER, that of Royal Arch discovers to the strict inquirer a *chasm*, the bottom of which, notwithstanding its native and artificial brilliancy, is enveloped in darkness."

So much being said in all the Degrees of Craft Masonry relative to the city of Jerusalem, it will be proper here to give a more complete account of that remarkable place. Its history surpasses in vicissitudes that of any other upon earth. Seventeen times has it been destroyed and rebuilt. Every nation that has risen in the Oriental world, for nearly four thousand years, has invested and captured Jerusalem, and in turn yielded it to succeeding spoilers. The first notice that history affords us of this remarkable place, is in the account of Abraham pursuing the four kings to Hobah, and rescuing his nephew Lot from their hands. Returning to Hebron, which was his residence, he was met in the Vale of Shaveh by Melchizedek, the king of Salem, to whom he paid tithes of the spoil he had captured. At the same time he received from that prince a blessing, even the blessing of the Most High God, together with such refreshments as his wearied party needed.

Upon the conquest of Palestine by Joshua, Jerusalem was cast to the lot of Benjamin; but the warriors of that tribe failing to seize it from the Jebusites, it fell to the people of Judah, upon whose boundary-line it stood, and whose superior prowess, under king David, wrested it from the hands of the enemy. David made it the Royal City and Metropolis of his kingdom. His son Solomon erected that wonderful and mysterious edifice, the Temple, upon its eastern eminence, Mount Moriah, and in the division of the kingdom, under Rehoboam, it remained the Metropolis of the Kingdom of Judah.

In the day of its highest splendor and prosperity its population exceeded a million of souls. The Jewish ceremonial requiring all the people to appear in the Temple three times a year, Jerusalem was ever a thronged city and the great inland mart of the nation. The surrounding hills, being terraced and irrigated, were covered with the fruitful things of that latitude, grains, figs, olives and vines. The cattle grazed upon the thousand hills, affording food, clothing, and wealth to the inhabitants.

But glorious as was the temporal prosperity shared with Tyre, Sidon, the cities of Egypt, and other flourishing emporiums, Jerusalem was more fortunate than any, in being the residence, the earthly home, of the Most High God. Jehovah, who had answered the supplications of King Solomon in the Fire and the Cloud, condescended to abide upon the Mercy-seat under the cherubim, in the Most Holy Place. By oracles, by the mystic Urim and Thummim, by visions, voices, and dreams, he answered the prayers of the faithful through the Divinely-ordained Priesthood, and made his presence known to those who rightly sought him. This fact, well understood by the pious Jews, made Jerusalem the "joy of the whole earth" to them. It was the Sacred City, the one spiritual oasis in a wilderness of heathen superstititions and impiety. From hence came forth the law. The Psalms of David were promulgated from this city. Ezra collated and composed the sacred canon here. Here for hundreds of years stood up, east of the Porch of the Temple, the grand pillars, Jachin and Boaz, the wonder and admiration of all beholders; an assurance to all, in their very names, that *in strength* God had covenanted *to establish* the honor, the city, the kingdom, the law forever, provided Israel would continue to serve him as their Lawgiver and Ruler.

Such, then, was the City of the Great King; the perfection of beauty, the joy of the whole earth. But, alas! how great has been her fall! How doth the city sit solitary that was full of people! how is she become as a widow!

Reft of thy sons, amid thy foes forlorn,
Mourn, widowed Queen! forgotten Sion, mourn!
Is this thy place, sad city, this thy throne,
Where the wild desert rears its craggy stone—
Where suns, unblest, their angry luster fling,
And way-worn pilgrims seek the scanty spring?
Where now thy pomp, which kings with envy viewed?
Where now thy might, which all these kings subdued?
No martial myriads muster in thy gate:
No suppliant nations in thy temple wait;
No prophet-bards, thy glittering courts among,
Wake the full lyre, and swell the tide of song;
But lawless force and meager want are there,
And the quick, darting eye of restless fear;
While cold oblivion, mid thy ruins laid,
Folds his dark wing beneath the ivy shade.

Jerusalem, now for more than a thousand years in possession of the infidel, is a miserable town, of less than ten thousand inhabitants, possessing not a wreck of its former glory. Temple, brazen pillars, palaces, all are gone. The very surface of the earth upon which pressed the feet of prophets, priests, and kings, is buried, in places, fifty feet deep beneath the *debris* of the former city, and, with the exception of a few great stones in the foundation-walls about Mount Moriah, it is impossible to point to an object fashioned by the hand of man, and affirmed with certainty, "this is the handiwork of the men of Solomon."

CRYPTIC MASONRY.—The term "Cryptic Masonry," as applied to the two Degrees of the Council, is derived more especially from the SELECT MASTER. Descriptions of some of the remarkable caves and substructures of King Solomon's Temple will be found upon subsequent pages. It is a pleasant tradition, illustrating this department, that the body of the Wise King yet lies entombed within a crypt, in the bowels of the Sacred Mountain, and that his spirit is permitted to wander forth at midnight, and to visit for *one hour* the places made memorable by his wisdom, valor, benevolence, or piety, during his lifetime. Among all these, however, there is none which his spirit haunts with such tenacity as *working Lodges of Freemasons.* Wherever Gavels ring or Jewels gleam, past the midnight hour, the spirit of Solomon is found, not visible to the eye, but apparent, it is said, to the well-informed, by the enlarged spirit of brotherly love animating every breast. The following lines illustrate the thought:

KING SOLOMON'S MIDNIGHT VISIT.

In a deep, rocky Cave great King Solomon lies,
Sealed up till the judgment from all prying eyes:
The Square on his breast, and his kingly brow crowned,
His Gavel and Scepter with filletings wound;
At midnight, impatient, his spirit comes forth,
And haunts for a season the places of earth.

He flits like a thought to the chambers of kings;
To the plain where black battle has shaken his wings;
To the cave where the student his late vigil keeps;
To the cell where the prisoner hopelessly weeps:
But most where Freemasons their mystical round
Continue past midnight, King Solomon 's found.

O, then when the bell tolls *low twelve*, do we hear
A rustling, a whispering startle the ear;

A deep solemn murmur, while Crafts stand in awe,
At something the eye of a mortal ne'er saw;
We know it, we feel it, we welcome the King,
Whose spirit takes part in the anthem we sing.

And then every heart beats responsive and warm;
The Acacia blooms freshly, we heed not the storm;
Our tapers are starlit, and lo! from above,
There seems as descending the form of a Dove!
'T is the Emblem of Peace that King Solomon sends,
To model and pattern the work of his friends.

His friends, loving brothers, when homeward you go
Bear Peace in your bosoms, let Peace sweetly flow!
In concord, in friendship, in brotherly love,
Be faithful, no emblem so true as the Dove;
The world will confess then, with cheerful accord,
You have met with King Solomon at midnight abroad!

THE TWENTY-SEVEN WORKMEN.

In the ranks of the faithful, whose biography is given with more or less minuteness in the Holy Scriptures, there are *Twenty-seven* names especially worthy the reverence of SELECT MASTERS. They are named below in the order of their lives. Each in his day performed his part, Trowel in hand, girded about with white raiment as becometh the faithful of God, to spread the cement upon the walls of moral architecture, and each is embalmed in the memory of all who revere virtue and fortitude devoted to a holy calling.

1. ADAM.—His birth was cotemporaneous with the creation of the world; he was the last and noblest of God's works. The victim of temptation, he was banished from Eden and condemned to a toilsome lot, which

he bore patiently, and thus, by faith in a coming Messiah, was reinstated in the favor of God. He died B. C. 3074, aged 930 years.

2. ABEL.—Born B. C. 4001, he met with a shocking death at his brother's hands at the age of 126 years. In his meekness, his piety, attention to religious duty, and undeserved death, he is an emblem of one "whose blood speaketh better things than that of Abel."

3. ENOCH.—Born B. C. 3382, he was translated beyond the persecutions of his enemies to the land of perpetual peace at the age of 365 years. "By faith Enoch was translated that he should not see death; and was not found because God had translated him; for before his translation he had his testimony that he pleased God."

4. NOAH.—Born B. C. 2948, this godly man, "being warned of God of things not seen as yet, moved with fear, prepared an ark to the saving of his house; by the which he condemned the world and became an heir of the righteousness which is by faith." He survived the flood 349 years, dying at the age of 950 years.

5. ABRAHAM.—This memorable character, the founder of the Jewish nation, was born in Chaldea, B. C. 1996, and died near Hebron, in Canaan, at the age of 175 years. "When called to go into a place which he should afterward receive for an inheritance, he obeyed; for he looked for a city which hath foundations, whose builder and maker is God."

6. ISAAC.—Born in the patriarchal abode at Beersheba, B. C. 1896, he lived a peaceable and quiet life, in the constant exercise of charity and benevolence, and died aged 180 years.

7. JACOB.—Born B. C. 1836, he lived a life of great vicissitudes, suffering much from the consequences of his own sins and the evil conduct of his children, yet ever trusting in God for pardon, and died in Egypt, in the arms of his beloved son Joseph, aged 147 years.

8. JOSEPH.—Born in Padan Aram, B. C. 1746, he was sold by his brothers as a slave, at the age of 17 years; was taken to Egypt and became its governor at the youthful age of 30. A model son and brother, he brought down all his relatives to Egypt, where he provided for their support, and died at the age of 110 years.

9. MOSES.—Born in a state of servitude in Egypt, B. C. 1571, he became at the age of 80 the Lawgiver and Captain of his people, whom he conducted by an arduous and devious route to the land of their fathers, and expired on Mount Pisgah, in view of the Promised Land, at the age of 120 years.

10. AARON.—Born in Egypt, B. C. 1574, he was the Deputy and Spokesman of his greater brother Moses; assisted him in conducting the people and putting into operation their new laws and ceremonials, and died upon Mount Hor, in Edom, at the age of 122 years.

11. JOSHUA.—Born in Egypt, B. C. 1553, he accompanied the spies from Kadesh Barnea into Canaan, was faithful amidst all disasters, and upon the death of Moses took command of the hosts of Israel, and accomplished the conquest of Palestine within about six years. He died, aged 110 years.

12. CALEB.—Born in Egypt, his career resembled that of Joshua. He was one of the spies who brought a good report to Moses. In the conquest of Canaan he fought a good fight, and was allotted Hebron and its surroundings for his inheritance.

13. BARAK.—A deliverer of Israel from the grievous oppressions of Sisera, he ruled his people in the fear of God for forty years.

14. GIDEON.—A follower in the chivalrous career of Barak, he rescued his country from the Midianites in a great battle at the well Harod, striking boldly in the name of the Lord.

15. JEPHTHAH.—The third in this band of national deliverers, he drove back the Ammonites, achieving a decisive victory at Aroer, and by his piety and valor gave peace to Israel, whom he ruled for six years.

16. SAMUEL.—Born at Ramathaim Zophim, B. C. 1155, he became the most eminent prophet and priest since the days of Moses. From early youth he had access to God, and by successive communications derived the Divine will by which he ruled his people Israel.

17. DAVID.—Born at Bethlehem, B. C. 1085, he was from his youth "a man after God's own heart." Though at times overcome by temptation, his sins were not presumptuous; he submitted patiently to punishment, and poured forth his penitence and thanksgiving in his deathless Psalms. He died at the age of 71 years, and was buried on Mount Sion, where his sepulcher is shown to this day.

18.—SOLOMON.—Born B. C. 1033, he is the Founder of Speculative Masonry or Freemasonry, of which his Temple on Mount Moriah was equally the spiritual and the practical model. He was emphatically the Wise King, the Moralist, the Royal Patron of Science and the Arts. Led into shocking follies, his old age recalled him to a purer life, and he died, it may be hoped, in the prospect of a better world.

19. HIRAM, KING OF TYRE.—The royal friend and provider of King Solomon, the Great Temple at Jerusalem was equally indebted to his munificent procurement of materials and his experienced skill in their distribution.

20. HIRAM, THE BUILDER.—The Operative Grand Master and companion of two kings, was "a widow's son of the tribe of Naphtali, filled with all wisdom and understanding, and cunning to work all works in brass; skillful to work in gold, and in silver, and in brass, in iron, in stone, and in timber, in purple, in blue, and in fine linen, and in crimson; also to grave any manner of graving, and to find out every device which shall be put

to him." This is the man whose noble death in defense of his integrity stands as a Masonic example to all ages.

21. ADONIRAM.—This man was the royal Treasurer of Solomon, and an active participant in the erection of the mystic temple of Freemasonry.

22. ELIJAH.—The Tishbite of Gilead stands foremost in the Old Testament Scriptures for nearness of access to the throne of Deity, for boldness of approach to kings, for powers of enduring hunger, thirst, and fatigue when upon the mission of God, and for the splendor of his departure, on one of the summits of Abarim, "in a chariot of fire and with horses of fire."

23. ELISHA.—The son of Shaphat, of Abel Meholath, became the successor of Elijah and the possessor of his mantle. He enjoyed, like him, the manifest favor of God. His miraculous powers proved his favor with Deity, which he ever exerted for the benefit of suffering humanity. In his day the nation of Israel, long divided into two kingdoms, was fast hastening, by a course of idolatry and sin, to its own destruction, an event that might be delayed, but could not be prevented by all the efforts of these prophets.

24. ZERUBBABEL.—A prince of the house of David, one of the captivity, who had kept his apron unspotted during the years of his exile, it was his happy portion to lead back the first portion of Judah to the land of their fathers. The destruction of Jerusalem by Nebuchadnezzar occurred B. C. 588. Zerubbabel, with his follow-

ers, reached the ruined city fifty-two years afterward, laid the foundation of the second Temple two years later, and dedicated it B. C. 515, seventy-three years after its destruction.

25. EZRA.—Coming from Babylon to Jerusalem, he was made governor, B. C. 457, and acted in that capacity for twelve years. He then became engaged in collecting and publishing the Jewish Scriptures, and restoring the purity of the Jewish worship.

26. JUDAS MACCABÆUS.—Made governor of Judea, B. C. 166, this man was the last of a long array of holy and valiant men who upheld their nation, always struggling against the greatest odds, preserved their religion from total destruction, and left upon record examples of undying interest.

27. JOHN THE EVANGELIST.—Born by the Sea of Galilee, and accustomed to the hardships and poverty of a fisherman's life, this man was raised, by faith in the Son of God, to the most commanding eminence among the Sons of Light. For his amiability he was styled "the beloved Disciple." After the tragedy upon Calvary he took charge of Mary, the mother of Jesus. He bore exile and tortures unflinchingly for Christ's sake, and expired at the ripe age of 100 years, the last and greatest of the Apostles.

These are the Twenty-seven whose names and history gleam forth from the pages of Scripture as the sun-rays from the eastern horizon, and who afford the laborers of the Trowel every shade of example which human exigencies can demand.

CHRONOLOGY OF THE SCRIPTURES.

It is essential to the understanding of Bible facts that a careful and accurate table of chronological data should be accessible to the reader. Such a one is here appended:

B. C.
4004—Creation of the World.
4002—Birth of Cain.
4001—Birth of Abel.
3875—Murder of Abel.
3874—Birth of Seth.
3382—Birth of Enoch.
3317—Birth of Methusaleh.
3074—Death of Adam.
3017—Translation of Enoch.
2962—Death of Seth.
2948—Birth of Noah.
2468—The Deluge threatened.
2348—Death of Methusaleh.
2348—The Flood.
2347—Termination of the Flood.
2234—Building of Babel.
2234—Confusion of Tongues and Dispersion.
2233—Nimrod began the Assyrian Monarchy.
2188—Mizraim began the Egyptian Monarchy.
1998—Death of Noah.
1996—Birth of Abraham.
1936—Abraham called to Haran.
1921—Abraham called to Canaan.
1913—Abraham's Victory over the Kings.
1910—Birth of Ishmael.
1897—God's Covenant with Abraham.

B. C.
1896—Birth of Isaac.
1871—Isaac offered.
1859—Death of Sarah.
1856—Isaac marries Rebecca.
1836—Jacob and Esau born.
1821—Death of Abraham.
1759—Jacob went to Padan.
1746—Joseph born.
1739—Jacob returned to Canaan.
1729—Joseph sold as a Slave.
1716—Joseph made Governor of Egypt.
1716—Death of Isaac.
1706—Jacob removed to Egypt.
1689—Death of Jacob.
1636—Death of Joseph.
1574—Birth of Aaron.
1571—Birth of Moses.
1553—Birth of Joshua.
1531—Moses fled to Midian.
1491—Moses commissioned.
1491—Departure of Israelites from Egypt.
1490—The Law delivered on Sinai.
1452—Death of Miriam.
1452—Death of Aaron.
1451—Death of Moses.
1451—Israelites enter Canaan.
1443—Death of Joshua.
1155—Birth of Samuel.
1116—Death of Eli, the High-Priest.
1095—Saul anointed King.
1085—Birth of David.
1063—David anointed King.
1055—Death of Saul.
1048—David King over all Israel.
1047—Jerusalem made the Jewish Metropolis.
1033—Birth of Solomon.
1023—Death of Absalom.

B. C.
1015—Solomon crowned King.
014—Death of David.
004—Completion of the Temple.
975—Rehoboam King.
958—Abijah King.
955—Asa King.
614—Jehoshaphat King.
892—Jehoram King.
885—Ahaziah King.
878—Joash King.
839—Amaziah King.
810—Uzziah King.
758—Jotham King.
742—Ahaz King.
726—Hezekiah King.
698—Manasseh King.
643—Amon King.
641—Josiah King.
610—Jehoahaz King.
599—Jehoiachin King.
599—Zedekiah King.
588—Babylonian Captivity.
588—Destruction of Jerusalem.
538—Babylon taken by Cyrus.
536—Return of Captives to Jerusalem.
534—Foundations laid of Second Temple.
529—The work ordered to cease.
520—Favorable Decree by Darius.
518—Esther made Queen.
515—Second Temple completed.
510—Haman's Plot frustrated.
484—Xerxes King of Persia.
464—Artaxerxes Longimarius.
457—Ezra sent to govern Jerusalem.
423—Darius Nothus.
335—Alexander establishes the Grecian Empire.
332—Jaddus High-Priest.

B. C.
323—Death of Alexander.
320—Jerusalem taken by Ptolemacus Lagus.
277—Septuagint Version of Scriptures made.
170—Jerusalem taken by Antiochus Epiphanes.
166—Judas Maccabæus Governor.
161—Jonathan Governor.
135—John Hyrcanus.
107—Judas High-Priest and King.
63—Jerusalem taken by Pompey.
40—Herod the Great, King.
28—Augustus Cæsar Emperor of Rome.
18—Herod begins the Third Temple.
4—Birth of John the Baptist.
4—Birth of Jesus Christ.

A. D.
1—Birth of Jesus Christ.
12—Jesus visits Jerusalem.
18—Tiberias Emperor of Rome.
26—Pontius Pilate Governor of Judea
29—John the Baptist began his Ministry.
30—Jesus baptized by John.
33—Jesus was Crucified.
35—Martyrdom of Stephen.
36—Saul Converted.
38—Conversion of the Gentiles.
42—Herod Agrippa King of Judea.
44—James beheaded.
54—Nero Emperor of Rome.
63—Paul sent prisoner to Rome.
65—Commencement of Jewish War.
66—Death of Paul.
70—Destruction of Jerusalem by Titus.
71—The City and Temple razed to foundations.
79—Titus Emperor of Rome.
81—Domitian Emperor of Rome.
95—John banished to Patmos.
96—John wrote Apocalypse.

A. D.
97—John liberated from exile.
100—John died.

ANTIQUITY.—There are few subjects to which antiquity does not lend a charm. The meditative mind loves to dwell upon what bears the impress of ages long gone by. An indefinable charm lingers around aged things—the oak, through whose branches have whistled the winds of a thousand winters; the mountain, whose bald summit has warded off the thunderbolts of ages; the stately pile of art, whose arches have echoed the footsteps of untold generations—and enchains the spirit as if by some magic spell. They connect us with the past, and tinge the mind with the solemn hues that color the distant. They extort an homage from the beholder that few things can. He who possesses a feeling soul will linger amid such scenes and objects with a pleasure mixed with grateful awe.

And if such is the power of antiquity when connecting us with things inanimate, how much more potent does it become when connecting us with the society of living, sentient beings of like feelings with ourselves! How sensitive the chord, how profound the feelings it awakens there! We no longer feel ourselves existing only now, and as individuals, but to be living at each separate period of our society's duration, and to have our hearts swell with the feelings and our minds kindle with the thoughts of all our brethren before us. Is it strange, then, that the Freemason should read the history of his ancient brethren with emotions? that he should love his Order all the better for being ancient, and render it an homage profounder and more devotional on that account? Had it been worthless it could never have become old. Things worthless do not so outlast the wastings of time; do not triumph, age after age, over all the oppositions of power and intelligence, inflamed by untiring hostility.

These thoughts are suggested to our minds in taking a chronological view like that afforded by the tables above. Measuring back from the Evangelist John, we mark a long array of names of men who have left their "footprints on the sands of time," and whose lives have been living monuments of the teachings of Freemasonry. A Society that flourished in the times of a Solomon, a Zerubbabel, a John—a light that shone with equal brilliancy upon an Abraham, a Moses, a Samuel—is worthy of profoundest admiration, if only for its antiquity and its unchangeableness in a world so fickle as ours. To look at a table of eminent men in the earlier stages of history is to look upon the Freemasons' Roll.

The principles by which these fathers of the ancient Art were actuated were few, simple, sublime. They are all communicated, either in letter or spirit, in the Moral Law, the Ten Commandments. Upon these, as a basis, men of all nations, ages, faiths could harmonize, and can harmonize. To add new rules and injunctions to these is to destroy the very Society which it is proposed thus to amend. This the poet has truly expressed in the following lines:

The OLD is better; is it not the plan
By which the Wise in by-gone days contrived
To bind in willing fetters man to man
And strangers in a sacred nearness lived?

Is there in modern wisdom aught like that
  Which 'midst the blood and carnage of the plain
Can calm man's fury, mitigate his hate,
  And join disrupted friends in love again?

No: for three thousand years the smiles of heaven,
  Smiles on whose sunbeams comes unmeasured joy,
To this thrice-honored cement have been given,
  This bond, this covenant, this sacred tie:
It comes to us full-laden: from the tomb
  A countless host conspire to name its worth,
Who sweetly sleep beneath the Acacia's bloom
  And there is naught like Masonry on earth.

Then guard the venerable relic well;
  Protect it, Masters, from the unholy hand;
See that its emblems the same lessons tell
  Sublime, through every age and every land:
Be not a line erased; the pen that drew
  These matchless tracings was the Pen Divine:
Infinite wisdom best for mortals knew;
  God will preserve intact the grand design.

CATALOGUE

OF

JOHN SHERER'S MASONIC PUBLICATIONS.

1. SHERER'S MASONIC CARPETS.

These are of two sorts. The first is a Master's Carpet, 6 by 6½ feet in size, finished in map style, molding at top, with roller at bottom, diversified and rich in its colorings. The other presents the emblems of the Blue Lodge, Chapter and Council Degrees, the same size, 6 by 6½ feet, finished in the same manner,

These Carpets have been so long before the Masonic public, although from time to time greatly improved and beautified, that no further description is needed. Official recommendations have been extended in their favor by the Grand Lodges and Chapters of Arkansas, Florida, Georgia, Indiana, Illinois, Kentucky, Louisiana, Mississippi, North Carolina and Texas, while letters of approbation have been given by many such men as Finley M. King, Rob Morris, John Dove, James Evans, James M. Hall, Cornelius Moore, Nathan B. Haswell, Salem Town, Benj. Parke, Horace Goodwin, Philip Swigert.

2. SHERER'S MASONIC DEGREE BOOK.

This is a collection of emblematic plates, suitable for framing separately, or for binding in a volume. The size of each plate is 20 by 26 inches. They are from the finest lithographic drawings, printed in colors on the best plate paper. The correctness of their symbolisms and elegance of execution are vouched for by a long array of the intelligent brethren who have examined them. As a frontispiece, there is a magnificent engraving, size as above, of "Jerusalem Besieged by Titus," taken from Bartlett's "Walks about Jerusalem." This alone is worth the price of the whole volume, $5.

3. SHERER'S GEMS OF MASONRY,

Emblematic and Descriptive,

Giving the Historical and Scriptural Illustrations of the Emblems of Masonry in the first Seven Degrees, and including Fifty-four Odes by the best poets of the Craft. This volume might justly be styled the Mine of Masonic Beauties. It is an indispensable aid to the intelligent Master who would feed his lodge with the rich food of Masonic learning and truth. No other work ever published blends so much beauty and learning as this.

4. VIEW OF JERUSALEM AS BESIEGED BY TITUS.

This is a magnificent Lithograph, printed in colors in the best style of Sarony, admitted to be the best living Lithographer. He has pronounced it his *chef d'œuvre*, and no one will dispute the correctness of his judgment who has a glimpse of it. For a parlor ornament, it is perfection itself. For a Lodge, nothing is more appropriate.

The View is 20 by 26 inches in dimensions, and will be sent securely packed in a tin case to any part of the continent for $2 00.

5. VIEW OF SOLOMON'S TEMPLE,

Engraved at Boston, upon two steel plates—full dimensions, 24 by 42 inches—at a cost exceeding Two Thousand Dollars. This is the celebrated design of Chancellor Schott, of Hamburgh, and the most complete explication of the inspired account of the great FANE ever published. Nothing but an examination will give a full idea of the vast amount of instruction to be derived from this engraving; the border designs, of which there are eight, the subsidiary drawings below the main picture, of which there are four, and the Scripture and historical passages thickly interspersed, make it a perfect cyclopedia of the subject. Price, in sheets for framing, $2.00; colored and finished in map form, molding at top and roller at bottom, $3.00.

6. THE FREEMASON'S MONITOR,

By Thomas Smith Webb, with notes and running comment by Rob Morris. This edition of the old and standard author, whose production has so long maintained its place in public favor amid the competition of nearly a score of imitations, is rendered immensely more valuable by the learning and experience of the present Editor. Mr. Morris has brought all his knowledge of Masonic law and usage to bear in making this work an indispensable aid to Masters, Wardens, and Brethren throughout the great Fraternity,

7. MASONIC DIPLOMAS

Of the various Degrees and Orders of the Blue Lodge, Chapter, Council and Encampment. Those of the Lodge are in three languages, viz.: English, German and French. Those of the Chapter have the Spanish in addition, and the Council Diploma is appended. Those of the Encampment are in English.

All these publications, whether carpets, plates, books, or diplomas, will be forwarded by express or otherwise, as ordered, to any part of the United States or Canada. The trade supplied on usual terms.

Address, JOHN SHERER, Cincinnati, Ohio

8. SHERER'S MASONIC DEGREE BOOK

Of Ancient Craft Masonry, being a correct presentation of the emblems of the Blue Lodge Degrees. This is a volume of 16 plates, 18 by 22 inches, including the views of King Solomon's Temple and Jerusalem besieged by Titus. The whole is strongly and handsomely bound, and inclosed in a neat box, made for it, with a lock and key. Price $20.

12. THE WINDING STAIRS,

Or the Carpet of the Middle Chamber. These are prepared for use in the Middle Chamber in the Fellow Crafts' Degree. There are three in a set, painted on oil-cloth with all the emblems, rising stairs, &c., needful to prompt the Senior Deacon in the elegant Lecture of that ceremony. Price $

10. THE MASONIC LADDER,

Or, The Nine Steps to Ancient Freemasonry; being a practical exhibit in prose and verse of the moral precepts, traditions, scriptural instructions, and allegories of the Degrees of the Blue Lodge, Chapter and Council. This work is just out, and will, it is believed, give greater satisfaction than any Masonic production now in the market. It is a volume of over 300 pages, containing, among other original matter, 10 Poems, written expressly for the work. It is so written as to be acceptable to Masons in the Blue Lodge only, as well as those in the higher degrees, and even to persons not Masons. Every brother will do well to send for a copy of this valuable book. Price $1.50.

11. MASTER MASON'S DIPLOMA.

This is by far the most appropriate and elegant Diploma ever issued; it is universally admired, and graces many a brother's parlor. In size it is 20x27 inches. It is printed in tint on heavy plate paper, for framing.

The design is that of the Form, Support and Covering of the Lodge. The view from the South displays the Pillar of Beauty in majestic proportions; those of Wisdom and Strength being in perspective. Jacob peacefully slumbering on his mystic pillow, lies at the foot of the Celestial Ladder, along which angels pass and repass on errands of mercy. The heavenly bodies are in their appointed places. The surrounding objects are such as are appropriate to Oriental climes. The whole constituting a splendid picture. At the foot of each Pillar are seen the Jewels of the Master and Wardens respectively. Below it is appended the proper form of Diploma, having blanks for names, dates, etc., and for the lodge seal and photograph of the owner. Every Master Mason should have this Diploma. Price $2.00 per copy. The same design on a scale of 13x18 inches is furnished for $1.50. Orders from secretaries and tylers filled at reduced rates.

www.ingramcontent.com/pod-product-compliance
Lightning Source LLC
LaVergne TN
LVHW010239110826
845151LV00004B/1335